The Garlic Lovers' Cookbook

THE GARLIC LOVERS' COOKBOOK

from
GILROY

Garlic Capital of the World

Celestial Arts
Millbrae, California

Celestial Arts
231 Adrian Road
Millbrae, California 94030

First Printing, July 1980

Cover design: Linda Herman
Cover photograph: Robert R. Stein
Interior illustrations: Mike Nelson

Made in the United States of America

Library of Congress Cataloging in Publication Data

Gilroy Garlic Festival Committee.
    The garlic lovers cookbook.

    Includes index.
    1.   Cookery (Garlic)   I. Title.
TX819.G3G54   1980   641.6′526   80-66298
ISBN 0-89087-272-4 (quality pbk.)

1   2   3   4   5   6   7   86 85 84 83 82 81 80

Y̶ou could call the
town of Gilroy
fragrant and
friendly.
MARJORIE RICE
Copley News Service

DEDICATION

Garlic lovers everywhere have much in common, the joy of eating
and cooking with this marvelous seasoning, of course, and an appreciation of the wonderful lore that surrounds garlic, both historical
and medicinal. But even more than this, we share in the aura of garlic. We respond to this simple bulb's invitation to enjoy life's plea-
sures—to appreciate good food, good friends, and good times together.

In this spirit of conviviality, we have lovingly compiled this cookbook from time-tested and cherished recipes of local residents, pro-
fessional and amateur chefs of the area, from entries in Gilroy's First
Annual Great Garlic Recipe Contest and from the fresh garlic growers
and shippers and Gilroy's own garlic dehydration processing plants.

It is dedicated in friendship to garlic lovers the world over by the
citizens of Gilroy. We also extend a very personal invitation to each of
you to join us in Gilroy the first weekend in August each year for our
Garlic Festival. Join us in paying tribute to garlic . . . and to Gilroy,
Garlic Capital of the World!

ACKNOWLEDGMENTS

The Gilroy Garlic Festival Committee gratefully acknowledges the participation of garlic lovers and garlic neophytes through whose Herculean efforts this cookbook has been created.

For their contributions and support, our appreciation and thanks to:
Garlic Lovers' Cookbook Committee Members

Betty Angelino   Nori Goforth
Karen Christopher   Mary Mozzone
Fred Domino   Rose Emma Pelliccione
Tim Filice   Dale Springer
A. & D. Christopher Ranch
Caryl Saunders Associates
Fresh Garlic Association
Foremost Gentry International
Gilroy Foods, Inc.
Miller, Perrin, Domino, Giacalone & Ackerman, Attorneys at Law

A special thanks to the generous donors of the courtesy recipes, the recipe contest participants and the unheralded, behind the scenes, recipe testers (and their families) who tested, tasted and critiqued the recipes we herein offer for your cooking and eating pleasure.

We have, by no means, been able to present "everything you would like to know about garlic" because there are so many more exciting garlic recipes and tips tucked away in memories, recipe boxes and cupboard drawers in kitchens all over the world.

We invite each of you garlic fanciers who has a special recipe that you may, in the spirit of friendship, like to share, to participate in the next annual Great Garlic Recipe Contest and Cook-off. Watch the food section of your local newspaper for contest details.

As one enthusiastic food editor wrote, "the time has come for garlic to come storming out of the pantry closet."

We're doing our best. . .

Here's to more garlic in our lives!

Gilroy Garlic Festival Association Inc.
P.O. Box 2311
Gilroy, California 95020

Contents

Gilroy, California
Garlic Capital of
The World

... when the fragrance of garlic is stirred with the redolence of fresh tomatoes and onions as they are also processed and with the sun-kissed fog as it rolls into town, the community looks and smells as if it were about to be engulfed with a spicy spaghetti sauce bubbling over the hills to the west. What a way to go!

MIKE DUNNE, Sacramento *Bee*

In August of 1979 something remarkable happened in the small town of Gilroy, California, which made newspaper headlines nationwide. As one writer who covered the event described it a few days later, "Small Town Has A Big Bash," and big bash it was, indeed. Gilroy declared itself the undisputed "Garlic Capital of the World" and nearly 30,000 people came to share in the celebration.

Challenged by what were perceived as false claims of several European cities where garlic production did not equal one-tenth that of Gilroy, the local citizenry set out to impress the world of their town's garlic supremacy. Under the leadership of a steering committee of community leaders and endorsed by the Chamber of Commerce, the citizens staged two days of garlic-related festivities which left little, if any, doubt about Gilroy's right to be acclaimed the world's garlic capital.

But Gilroy was not always an eligible contender for the garlic crown. When first settled in the 1850s by disillusioned gold seekers who decided to try their hands at fortune of another sort, fruit trees were planted in the fertile soil and, eventually, Gilroy became distinguished for the fine quality of its fruit crops. During this period most

1

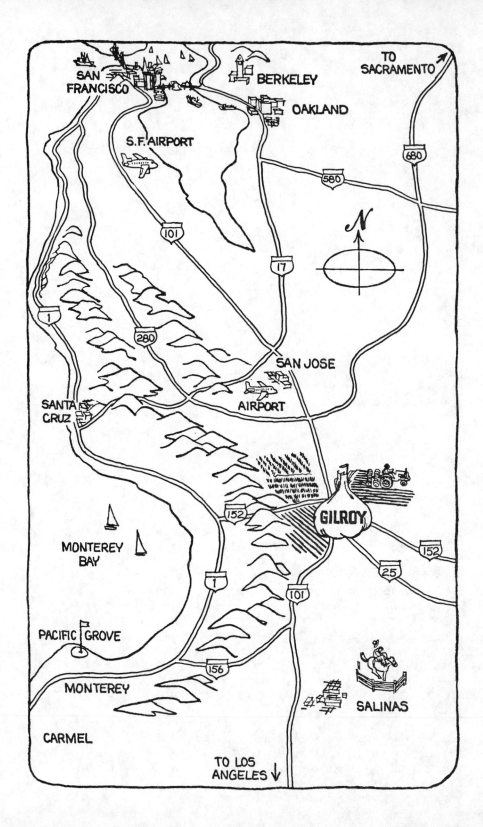

of the garlic consumed in the United States was imported from Europe. It wasn't until the 1920s that the first small garlic plantings were attempted in Gilroy.

Today most of the fruit trees have been replaced by vegetable row crops, including about 14,000 acres of garlic under cultivation in the 90-mile radius surrounding Gilroy. Nearly 150 million pounds of garlic are produced from this acreage. About 40 million pounds are sold on the fresh market, and the rest are dehydrated for use in a variety of consumer products: household seasonings, commercial flavoring for pickles, catsups, condiments, salad dressings, convenience foods and in a growing number of health aids.

The temperate climate of this small agricultural community, situated midway between San Francisco and the Monterey peninsula and just twelve miles or so from the Pacific Ocean, permits the production of many other fine crops such as onions, tomatoes, peppers and assorted fruits and vegetables. Some aromatic changes occur in the local atmosphere when the tomato canneries and the garlic and onion dehydrators are in operation simultaneously: the air for nearly ten miles around Gilroy takes on the quality of an Italian kitchen! Local residents claim it is simply impossible to resist the temptation to drop everything at such times and return home to stir up a pot of spaghetti sauce.

Will Rogers, according to local legend, said it even better. After driving through Gilroy at harvest time, he described it as "the only town in America where you can marinate a steak just by hanging it out on the clothesline."

Gourmet Alley

The most popular attraction, however, was Gourmet Alley, a crescent of food booths backed up against a wall of wind-breaking poplars behind the hacienda. Here (one saw) a fast-working, sweat-dappled crew running about a foundry-like outdoor kitchen of homemade barbecue grills and primitive gas-fired stoves.

The fare they were turning out, however, had all the style, appearance, texture, flavor and appeal of continental cuisine patiently cooked in the stainless-steel kitchen of a gourmet restaurant.

MIKE DUNNE, Sacramento Bee

The soaring American appetite for garlic (up more than 1000% in the past ten years) assures a garlicky future for Gilroy and promises perpetuation of the Garlic Festival, which has focused world attention on this central coastal California community.

The garlic festival has been described by a national columnist as a "true bit of Americana, where the whole town turns out" to make this spectacle happen. Local merchants, civic, social and charitable organizations as well as the farmers and processors themselves, provide exhibits and booths which offer information and garlic in every form from bulk to braids and from deodorized to dehydrated. The festival market displays everything imaginable with a garlic motif, including shirts, hats, belt buckles, jewelry, paperweights, plaques, drawings, books, and much more.

Free entertainment (there is a small entrance fee to the festival grounds) includes opera, minstrel and barbershop singers, rock bands, mimes, banjos, country and western music, acrobats and, for the young children, puppeteers, magicians and games. Other events associated with the festival help to round out the weekend—a Miss Garlic Beauty Pageant, an Open Golf Tournament, a Barn Dance and the Gilroy Garlic Gallop, a 10,000 meter race.

Garlic-topping contests are held to test the speed and skills of the harvesters who work in the industry. Contestants move expertly through the rows of pulled garlic, quickly removing the roots and dried "tops" with sharp hand shears. Tours of the garlic fields and packing and processing plants are popular and, since Gilroy is also wine country, trips to the local wineries include tastings of their proferred spirits.

A featured event of the festival is the Great Garlic Recipe Contest and Cook-off, where entrants who have eagerly vied for the opportunity to be among the finalists come to Gilroy to prepare their own favorite garlic dishes. The winners are chosen by a panel of illustrious judges selected from prominent newspaper and magazine food editors. Judges for the first contest included columnist and food critic, Anthony Dias Blue; food editor of *Bon Appetit* magazine, Rita Leinwand; food editors Marjorie Rice of the San Diego *Tribune* and Harvey Steiman of the San Francisco *Examiner;* and Shirley Sarvis, free lance food writer and consultant. The winning recipes are included and identified herein.

But the heart of the festival is "Gourmet Alley"—the outdoor kitchen where, for love and charity, about 50 local amateur chefs (including businesswomen, farmers, lawyers, bankers, housewives, and real estate brokers) prepare such garlic-laden delicacies as scampi, calamari, pasta con pesto, stuffed mushrooms, marinated pepper steak, and of course, huge slabs of aromatic garlic bread. During the First Garlic Festival, the cooks in "Gourmet Alley" served nearly 600 pounds of calamari, 300 pounds of scampi, 400 of pasta, 200 of mushrooms, 700 of meat, 250 of bell peppers, 750 loaves of French bread, all cooked with a whopping 300 pounds of fresh garlic! This was in addition to the delicious oysters in garlic sauce, gazpacho, chili, empanadas, quesadillas and all the other fabulous food served at the festival.

How is it possible for a small community to muster so much volunteer talent and dedication? To expect the chefs and their families, as well as the other townspeople, to labor all weekend in order to provide festival goers with such memorable food and entertainment? Ah......to grasp this, one must first understand the phenomenon that is Gilroy.

Actually the name "Gourmet Alley" could just as easily be applied to Gilroy itself. Not only is such a large percentage of the fresh and dehydrated seasoning associated with good cooking produced here, but the people themselves, many of whom boast a strong Mediterranean cultural heritage, are dedicated to good food and its preparation.

Inspired by the diversity of crops produced in their own community and the fragrant "fallout" during the harvest season, the residents also have access to the bountiful seafood from nearby Monterey Bay. Unlike the harvest festivals of other agricultural areas in California, which customarily take the form of a western-style steak or chicken barbecue, those held in the Gilroy area offer clams, mussels, calamari, and pasta dishes in addition to the more traditional foods. And it is not at all unusual for the men of Gilroy to get together

to make sausage or to taste the newest recipe for spaghetti sauce or even develop an exciting new recipe for a garlic hors d'oeuvre during a hunting expedition. There's just such a recipe in this book!

In Gilroy the men take pride in their culinary accomplishments and consider it a great honor if asked to be one the chefs of "Gourmet Alley." Much good natured controversy has developed over who makes the best marinara sauce or whose scampi has the most delicate flavor. Recipes are jealously guarded. The women of Gilroy share their husbands' delight in matters gastronomic and many make a dedicated effort to preserve and pass on to their young people a sense of pride and appreciation of the recipes and techniques for preparing food as a part of their cultural legacy.

"Gourmet Alley" really had its beginning long before the concept of a Garlic Festival was a reality. But it is the Festival which has provided an international showcase for the talents of the townspeople of Gilroy. And it is the Festival which has made this cookbook a possibility and enabled its editors to wrest so many cherished (and most secret) recipes from the chefs of Gilroy. For that we can all be grateful.

Gilroy held its First Annual Garlic Festival last week, and Lloyd Harris explained: "There's something about garlic that creates excitement. People can get real loose around garlic."

Time Magazine

Garlic History and Mystery

Throughout history, as today, garlic was either revered or reviled, depending upon one's personal taste and the dictates of society. One of the oldest of cultivated plants and a member of the lily family, along with onions, chives, shallots and leeks, it was known in "Olde English" as *garleac*. Its scientific name is *allium sativum*, which has given rise to the term alliumphiles or garlic lovers—those for whom this cookbook will hold particular allure.

The garlic plant has flat, grayish green leaves which grow to be one or two feet tall, but the part of the plant revered in song and story and treasured over the centuries is the bulb. Mentioned over 5000 years ago in the first written language, Sanskrit, garlic was a staple in the ancient Sumerian diet. According to the Greek historian, Herodotus, Egyptian workers who built the Pyramid of Cheops refused to work without their daily portion of garlic. Garlic was even found entombed with King Tutankhamun.

Garlic is known to have been planted in the gardens of the King of Babylon and Homer praised it for its health-giving properties. Greek gladiators, and later Roman soldiers, girded themselves for battle with doses of garlic from which they expected to derive both strength and courage. The Romans also considered it an aphrodisiac which is why, some think, they ate so much of it.

Thought to have originated in Siberia, its culture spread widely, and Marco Polo, among others, mentioned the many uses of garlic in records of his journeys. Crusaders, returning to Europe from their battles in the Holy Land, are credited with introducing garlic to that continent, where at one time it was so popular that banquet guests were requested to compose verses saluting it. In Boccaccio's *Decameron*, a love-stricken young man sent garlic to his lady in order to win her love . . . and he did!

THE MAGIC OF GARLIC

Undoubtly because of its potent scent and flavor, in ancient times garlic was thought to have mystical properties and was used as a defense against both known and unknown evils. Even today there are those who hang wreaths of garlic about their houses or single cloves about their necks to guard against sinister spirits, and in some cultures it is still considered a sign of great good fortune to dream of garlic.

The custom in Balkan countries was to rub garlic on doorknobs and window frames to discourage vampires, and runners chewed garlic to keep competitors from getting in front of them.

But legend is not all on the positive side. A Mohammedan folktale explains that when Satan was ejected from the Garden of Eden, garlic sprang up wherever he set down his feet, and in 1330 King Alfonso XI of Castile is said to have founded a knightly order based entirely on hatred of garlic.

THE ORIGINAL PANACEA: MEDICINAL FOLKLORE

But what about garlic's curative powers? In antiquity a common name for garlic was "cure-all," and through the centuries this simple bulb has steadfastly maintained its reputation for healing everything from simple infection to high blood pressure and tuberculosis.

The ancient Greeks and Romans prescribed garlic for hundreds of specific ailments. On the other hand, in the sixteenth century, Parisians were promised good health the year 'round if they would but eat garlic with fresh butter during the month of May. The British actually used garlic to control infection during World War I, and the Russians used it to control rampaging flu epidemics.

Truly, there is more lore surrounding the tiny clove of garlic than around any other food. Folk medicine says that a cold will surely be cured if one rubs the soles of the feet with cut cloves of garlic. For toothache, there are two schools of thought; one, that a sliver of garlic placed in the cavity of the tooth will relieve the ache; the other says that the sufferer should place a slice of garlic in the ear. For earache, a cut clove is rubbed over and around the ear.

G ILROY'S
BREATHTAKING
CELEBRATION
Vacaville *Reporter*

History records that King Henry V was anointed at birth with wine and garlic because it was believed that garlic on a baby's lips served as a stimulant and antiseptic. One might argue here more in favor of the wine. But Millin, writing in 1792, praised garlic as a preventive against the plague, and Bernardin de Saint-Pierre recorded that garlic cured nervous maladies.

Scientific proof or no, the belief that garlic can "cure what ails you" persists and, in fact, seems to be on the increase. But whether or not medical science ever reaches any definite conclusions about the curative powers of garlic seems of little consequence to true garlic lovers. Most important is the magic which garlic performs in the kitchen. The delicious flavors that result from blending garlic with other foods can only be described as pure witchcraft.

Good Things to Know About Garlic

Like most other important foods, there are certain basic things to know about garlic. The following information has been assembled to help you identify the various forms of garlic found on the commercial market and make better use of them in your cooking.

SELECTION AND STORAGE

Fresh garlic, which may be creamy white or have a purplish-red cast, should be plump and firm, with its paperlike covering intact—not spongy, soft or shriveled. Store in a cool, dry place with adequate ventilation. Refrigeration is not recommended. However, if fresh garlic must be kept for a long time, it can be peeled and the whole cloves dropped into olive oil and stored in the refrigerator for as long as three months. Garlic which is held in open-air storage for any length of time will lose much of its pungency. If it does, or if sprouts develop, the garlic is still usable, but it will be somewhat milder, and more may be needed to achieve the same strength of flavor in the dish being prepared.

Dehydrated forms of garlic should be purchased in tightly sealed containers, preferably from markets where there is sufficient traffic and turnover to ensure that the spices are fresh. Store with other spices in as cool and dry a place as possible, definitely not above or next to the kitchen range, sink, or in front of a window with exposure to the sun. Keep tightly sealed.

PEELING AND COOKING TECHNIQUES

Peeling garlic can be a problem. One way is to press each clove against the cutting board with the flat side of a heavy kitchen knife. Or pour hot water over the cloves for just a few seconds. This will loosen the skin and allow it to be pulled off easily with a paring knife. The cloves may also be soaked in cool water for about a half hour before peeling. Or put in a microwave oven for 5 seconds or so.

When cooking garlic in hot oil, remember that it burns easily and when burned, the flavor is not as palatable. When garlic is cooked for a long time, it becomes very mellow and nut-like in flavor and can be spread on bread and potatoes like butter.

Garlic flavors foods differently, depending on how it is used. It is most pungent when eaten raw, especially crushed or minced. Whole cloves or large pieces will give off a gentler flavor.

Garlic is very low in calories. Each clove of fresh garlic contains only one to two calories and can be used without concern for many dietary dishes. It is especially good as a flavoring in low-sodium diets.

The flavor of garlic is unusually good in dishes which contain onions.

ODOR

Fresh parsley, or other foods high in chlorophyll content, will help to prevent garlic odor on the breath. Parsley has been called "nature's mouthwash."

To remove the odor of garlic from the hands, rub with salt or lemon juice and then rinse under cold water. Repeat if necessary. If the odor of garlic or onions has permeated a plastic bowl or storage container, wash thoroughly, then crumple a piece of newspaper, add to container and cover tightly. Odor should disappear within a few days.

FRESH/DEHYDRATED GARLIC EQUIVALENTS

Fresh and dehydrated garlic may be used interchangeably; it's a matter of the cook's preference. To assist in converting recipes from one form to the other we offer the following equivalents:

1 average-size clove   = 1/8 teaspoon dehydrated
  fresh garlic   powdered, minced or
                               chopped garlic

1 average-size clove   = 1/2 teaspoon garlic salt.
  fresh garlic   (Caution: when using
                               garlic salt in recipes
                               calling for fresh garlic,
                               decrease the amount of
                               salt called for.)

RECOMMENDED USE PROPORTIONS

As cooks become more confident in the use of garlic and discover what wonders its flavor can perform with simple meat and vegetable dishes, they tend to use larger and larger quantities. For the beginner, who may be uncertain about how much garlic to use when experimenting with familiar recipes, we offer the following proportions of fresh or dehydrated garlic. Keep in mind that these are on the low side and most who really enjoy the flavor of garlic will want to use a great deal more.

Meats: For each 2 pounds of pork, beef, lamb or other meats, use 1/8 to 1/4 teaspoon garlic powder, or 1 1/2 to 2 teaspoons garlic salt, or 2 or 3 cloves fresh garlic.

Sauces: For 3 cups barbecue, tomato or other sauce, use 1/8 to 1/4 teaspoon garlic powder or 2 or 3 cloves fresh garlic.

Soups: To 3 cups meat stock or vegetable soup, add 1/8 teaspoon garlic powder, or 2 cloves fresh garlic.

Pickled foods: Per quart of kosher-style dill pickles or per pint of dilled green beans, add 1/8 to 1/4 teaspoon dehydrated chopped or minced garlic or 2 to 3 cloves fresh garlic.

Relishes: To 2 pints of chutney or relish, add 1/8 teaspoon dehydrated minced garlic, or 2 cloves fresh garlic.

Appetizers/Antipasti

In medieval times, garlic was considered to be a remedy for loss of appetite. In the 20th century garlic still is revered for the same attribute. Consider the delectable morsels we serve at the beginning of a meal—escargots, bagna cauda, and garlic stuffed mushrooms, to name a few. These fragrant garlic goodies start the meal with a burst of flavor to whet the appetite and provide inspiration and anticipation.

QUICK AND EASY APPETIZERS

For an easy cheese spread, combine cream cheese, grated sharp cheese, seasoned salt and minced garlic with enough mayonnaise to moisten. Shape into a ball or log and roll in chopped nuts. Serve with crackers.

You can make aioli—the French garlic mayonnaise—in a hurry. To a cup of ordinary mayonnaise, add 2 or 3 finely chopped fresh garlic cloves. Serve as a dip for vegetables or as a sauce for meats or fish.

Stuff ripe or green pitted olives with almonds. Place stuffed olives in a jar with liquid from kosher or spicy pickles and 5 or 6 cloves of fresh garlic. Chill for 24 hours.

Spinach dip is lovely with crackers or vegetable sticks. Cook a package of frozen spinach, squeezing out water. Add chopped green onions, minced parsley, two cloves of minced garlic and enough mayonnaise to make thick dip consistency. Add salt to taste.

Peel fresh garlic cloves and saute in a small amount of oil sprinkled with oregano. Turn often until well browned. Drain on paper towels and sprinkle with coarsely ground salt. Serve warm for nibbling with cold beverages.

19

"Smell that!" Mike Filice commanded, then thrust his own nose into his 30 clove garlic sauce. "Heaven on earth!"

ELIZABETH MAHREN, Oakland *Tribune*

ANTIPASTO AGLIO   *Garlic Antipasto*

This wonderful and imaginative appetizer is the creation of one of Gilroy's finest amateur chefs who devised it for his companions on a hunting trip. When prepared this way, garlic's assertive flavor is diminished to a delicate, nut-like taste. The recipe was selected as a finalist in the First Great Garlic Recipe Contest.

Recipe contest finalist: M. J. Filice, Gilroy

30 large cloves fresh garlic
1 2 oz. can fillets of anchovies
1 tbsp. finely chopped parsley
1 tbsp. butter, melted
1 tbsp. olive oil
Dash Tabasco
¼ cup olive oil
Sardine French bread, 2 or 3 dozen thinly sliced and toasted pieces. (Sardine is a long, thin bread also called "flute." Available in most markets.)

Peel garlic cloves and slice centers ⅛ inch thick. Press ends through garlic press to yield ¼ tsp. Place pressed garlic in small bowl with anchovies. Add parsley, butter, 1 tsp. oil, and Tabasco; mash to a paste. Cover and refrigerate. Heat ¼ cup oil, add garlic slices and saute to a light golden brown—almost to a potato chip fry. *Do not overfry!* Spread anchovy paste on toast. Garnish with garlic slices and WHAM-O!—the taste of tastes! Follow with a sip of robust red wine. *Salute e buon appetito!!*

DAVE'S FAVORITE GARLIC DIP

Everyone likes garlic dip, and sometimes the simpler it is the better it is. Serve this with chips or crackers or use to stuff celery. Great!

Recipe contest entry: Lois Biggs, Gilroy

1 8 oz. package cream cheese
3 tbsp. milk
5 large cloves fresh garlic
Salt
Parsley
Paprika

With fork, mix cream cheese and milk in small bowl until it has the texture of peanut butter. Press garlic and add to cream cheese mixture. Salt to taste and mix thoroughly. Garnish with parsley and paprika. Refrigerate until ready to use.

GARLIC GUACAMOLE

This is no ordinary guacamole! It's a unique variation. Once you start eating it you won't stop until you've scraped the bowl clean.

Recipe contest entry: Chris Ursich, San Mateo

1 ripe California avocado
1/8 lb. tofu, firm-style (found in fresh produce section of most supermarkets)
4 to 6 cloves fresh garlic
1/2 medium-sized bell pepper
2 green onions
2 tbsp. freshly chopped parsley
1/2 tsp. curry powder
1/2 tsp. oregano
1/2 tsp. thyme
1/4 tsp. freshly ground black pepper
4 to 6 tbsp. hot sauce
Juice of 1/2 lime (or lemon)
Tortilla chips for dipping

Mash avocado and tofu in bowl. Squeeze garlic through press and add. Finely chop bell pepper and green onion and stir in. Add herbs and spices. Mix well. Add hot sauce. Stir in lime juice. Eat with tortilla chips. Garlic Guacamole can be refrigerated, but do not make more than a few hours in advance.

EGGPLANT DIP SOLANO

Everyone who has tried this says it's great for a company dish, and inexpensive as well.

Recipe contest entry: Ruth Solano, San Jose

1 eggplant
1/4 onion, minced
3 cloves garlic, minced or pressed
Olive oil
Salt and pepper to taste

Cook eggplant in heavy skillet over low flame, turning frequently until skin is dark and crackles to the touch. Cool, peel and mash pulp; add onion and garlic. Add oil, a little at a time, while continuing to mash pulp, until mixture is creamy in texture. Eggplant absorbs the oil, so quite a bit is needed. Add salt and pepper to taste. Refrigerate. May be used as a dip for vegetables or on chunks of pita bread as a spread.

"TOO EASY"

A good spread to put together in a hurry when friends or family arrive unexpectedly.

Courtesy of: Doris Lane, Gilroy

2 cups grated Cheddar cheese
¼ cup (approx.) mayonnaise
1 clove fresh garlic, minced fine
1 tsp. dehydrated parsley flakes

Combine grated cheese, mayonnaise and garlic. Mix well. Be sure it is moist. Increase mayonnaise if necessary. Refrigerate for awhile to allow flavors to mingle. When ready to serve spread mixture on muffins or French bread and broil until cheese is melted. Garnish with parsley. May be served with rye crackers.

BAGNA CAUDA

The name of this sauce, a specialty of the Piedmont region of Italy, literally means "hot bath." Keep it hot by serving from chafing dish.

6 large cloves fresh garlic
1 cup sweet butter
¼ cup olive oil
2 tbsp. chopped anchovies
Vegetables and bread sticks for dipping

Peel garlic and mince fine or put through garlic press. Melt butter in small sauce pan. Add garlic and oil. Cook over very low heat 5 minutes until garlic is softened but not browned. Add anchovies and continue cooking 5 minutes. Serve as a dip for raw or lightly blanched vegetables such as cucumber, fresh mushrooms, celery, zucchini, carrots, cauliflower, green pepper and green onions and bread sticks. *Variation:* Blend 1 cup whipping cream and a generous dash or two freshly ground pepper into garlic-butter mixture. Simmer 2 or 3 minutes. Serve while warm.

We are confident that the spirit of the Gilroy Garlic Festival will linger on.
San Jose *Mercury*

SLENDER CHEESY SPREAD

There's no joy in being on a diet, but if you have a few favorite low-calorie standby recipes, you can usually make it through the difficult times when you just "have to have something" without going too far over your calorie limit. Try this cheesy spread with all kinds of vegetables or diet crackers. *Recipe contest entry: Mrs. Gilbert Blakey, San Clemente*

1 pt. 4% fat cottage cheese
3 cloves fresh garlic,
  minced
1 tbsp. finely chopped
  parsley
1 tbsp. mayonnaise
1 tbsp. wine vinegar
  Salt and pepper to taste
  Celery salt to taste

Mix all ingredients together, cover and refrigerate overnight. Use to stuff celery, scooped-out small zucchini halves or to spread on crackers or wedges of toast. Sprinkle tops with paprika for added color.

CALIFORNIA CRAB DIP

California is well-known not only for its garlic but for the local crab, called Dungeness. You don't have to be a Californian to prepare this unusual and pleasing crabmeat combination. Canned or frozen crabmeat can be substituted if fresh is not available.

1 cup crabmeat (fresh,
  canned or frozen)
1/4 cup lime juice (or lemon)
1 3 oz. package cream
  cheese
1/4 cup heavy cream
2 tbsp. mayonnaise
1 tsp. instant minced onion
1 tsp. shredded green
  onion
1 tsp. Worcestershire sauce
1/2 tsp. salt
1/4 tsp. garlic powder
1/8 tsp. MSG (optional)
2 dashes cayenne or red
  pepper

Marinate crabmeat in lime (or lemon) juice 30 minutes. Beat together cream cheese, cream, mayonnaise and seasonings until smooth and creamy. Fold in marinated crabmeat. For an attractive presentation, serve in a deep shell or shell-shaped bowl nested in crushed ice with an interesting arrangement of bite-sized pieces of Chinese cabbage, celery, sliced cauliflowerets, green pepper strips and thin slices of carrot. Don't forget a basket of crackers or chips! Makes about 1 1/2 cups.

MARION AND LINDA'S BAKED STUFFED CLAMS

Rated excellent by all who have tried them, these stuffed clams can be made ahead, frozen and popped in the oven just half an hour before serving time.   *Recipe contest entry: Marion Molnar and Linda Hussar, Gilroy*

8 slices bacon
1½ tbsp. oil
3 cloves fresh garlic, minced
2 tbsp. chopped parsley
1 tbsp. chopped onion
⅓ cup plus 2 tbsp. dry bread crumbs
Pinch of oregano
Dash of pepper
Salt, if necessary, but very little
2 cups chopped clams, fresh-steamed or canned
⅔ cup clam liquid
3 tbsp. grated Parmesan cheese

Render fat from bacon, and reserve 1½ tablespoons drippings. Drain on paper towels. Combine drippings and oil in pan and gently saute garlic, parsley, and onion. Add ⅓ cup bread crumbs, oregano, pepper, and salt if needed. Heat not more than three minutes. Add clams and clam liquid and mix well. Spoon into individual baking dishes or clean clam shells. Sprinkle with cheese and remaining bread crumbs. Dust with paprika and sprinkle with pieces of reserved bacon. Bake at 350°F about 25 minutes or until tops are brown and bacon crisp. Baking time will depend on the size of serving. Stuffed clams may be made ahead of time and frozen, then baked 35 minutes. Makes 4 to 6 servings.

SHRIMP APPETIZER SUPREME

This excellent shrimp appetizer could be served as a main dish with either rice or noodles.   *Recipe contest entry: Susan Strommer, Los Angeles*

2 lbs. extra-large shrimp
1 tsp. salt
½ tsp. pepper
4 tbsp. lemon juice
3 cloves fresh garlic, crushed
4 tbsp. mayonnaise
1½ cups fine dry bread crumbs
1 tsp. crushed basil leaves
2 tsp. chopped parsley
½ tsp. dill weed
½ cup melted butter
4 tbsp. olive oil

Shell and devein shrimp. Mix salt, pepper, lemon juice, garlic and mayonnaise. Stir in shrimp and refrigerate for 1 to 2 hours. Mix bread crumbs, basil, parsley and dill. Coat each shrimp with crumbs and place in single layer in shallow baking dish. Stir melted butter and olive oil into remaining marinade. Pour over shrimp. Bake at 400°F for 15 minutes. Makes 6 to 8 servings.

ZUCCHINI APPETIZER ANGELINO

Italian squash, zucchini, is abundant the year 'round and is usually reasonably priced, which makes it a good choice to help keep the budget in line when entertaining. The aroma while this dish bakes is so good, your family or guests will be waiting expectantly for their first taste!   *Courtesy of: Betty Angelino, Gilroy*

4 cups unpeeled zucchini, grated
1¾ cups biscuit mix
¾ cup Parmesan cheese
½ cup vegetable oil
4 eggs, beaten
1 large onion, chopped or grated
3 cloves fresh garlic, minced
3 tbsp. minced parsley
½ tsp. salt
½ tsp. oregano, crushed

Combine all ingredients in large mixing bowl and stir until well blended. Spread in greased baking dish 13x9x2. Bake in preheated 350°F oven for 25 to 30 minutes until golden brown. Cut into bite-sized serving pieces. May be served hot or cold.

PARSLEY-GARLIC FINGER SANDWICHES

Parsley and garlic are good friends. The chlorophyll in the parsley helps to prevent the odor of garlic on the breath. Combined with mayonnaise as a spread, the two herbs make very tasty finger sandwich appetizers.   *Recipe contest entry: Mrs. George Parrish, Gilroy*

2 bunches finely chopped parsley
2 large cloves fresh garlic, pressed
½ cup mayonnaise
1 large loaf extra-thin white bread, crusts removed

Combine parsley, garlic and mayonnaise; mix well. Spread mixture between two slices of bread and cut diagonally to make four finger sandwiches. Refrigerate until ready to use. These can be made early on the day to be used, but *not* the day before.

ZUCCHINI AND MUSHROOM HORS D'OEUVRES

With everyone trying to eat more nutritious foods and avoid "empty calories," this healthful, delicious and simple-to-prepare company hors d'oeuvre should help to make you a popular host or hostess.

Recipe contest entry: Linda Tarvin, Morgan Hill

½ cup butter or margarine
4 cloves fresh garlic, minced
2 tbsp. chopped parsley
Pepper
1 lb. mushroom caps
2 medium-sized zucchini, sliced ¼ inch thick
Parmesan cheese
Paprika

Combine butter, garlic, parsley and cook until bubbly. Add pepper to taste and then chill slightly so that mixture is not runny. Arrange mushrooms, cupped side up, and zucchini slices on serving dishes. Top caps and slices with ¼ teaspoon garlic butter mixture. Sprinkle with Parmesan cheese and paprika. Cook 1 to 2 dozen at a time for 2 to 4 minutes under broiler.

ESCARGOTS CARMELA

What garlic cookbook would be complete without a recipe for garlic-buttered snails? This variation was an entry in the First Great Garlic Recipe Contest and Cook-off. You might try a light sprinkling of Parmesan cheese on each snail before baking. Serve with plenty of hot French bread to sop up the garlic butter!

Recipe contest entry: Carmela M. Meely, Walnut Creek

4 oz. butter, softened
1 tbsp. chopped parsley
3 cloves fresh garlic, minced
1 minced shallot
Pepper
Salt
Pinch ground nutmeg
1 tbsp. white wine or champagne
1 dozen snails and shells

Cream butter; add all ingredients, except snails, and mix until well-blended. Put a bit of butter into each snail shell; add snails and cover each with a dollop of butter mixture. Bake at 350°F for 10 minutes. Makes 1 dozen.

ITALIAN SAUSAGE STUFFED MUSHROOMS

Italians everywhere love their mushrooms. Some like them best as an appetizer stuffed with garlic and Italian sausage.

Recipe contest entry: Carmela M. Meely, Walnut Creek

18 to 20 large mushrooms
½ lb. Italian sausage (regular or fennel, bulk type)
½ cup chopped onion
3 cloves fresh garlic, minced
3 tbsp. oil
¼ cup bread crumbs
1 egg
¼ cup grated Parmesan cheese
Additional Parmesan cheese for garnish

Remove stems from mushrooms. Chop stems. Brown sausage, onion, garlic and chopped stems in oil. Drain well. Cool. Mix with bread crumbs, egg, cheese. Stuff mushrooms full. Bake at 350°F for 15 to 20 minutes. Sprinkle with extra Parmesan. Makes about 6 appetizer servings.

Linda Tarvin's recipe for Garlic Toothpaste for Yellow and/or Stained Teeth didn't make it to the Great Garlic Cook-off finals. It called for 20 cloves of garlic. However, the toothpaste recipe did provide a few laughs for the committee sorting the 500-plus entries. And that was the retired teacher's intent. "Does not remove yellow or stain from teeth but nobody will ever get close enough to notice," says Mrs. Tarvin.

MARY PHILLIPS, San Jose *Mercury*

GARLIC MUSHROOMS MORGAN HILL

Linda was among the top ten finalists in the First Great Garlic Recipe Contest and her mushroom recipe drew raves not only for its flavor but for its attractive presentation with whole garlic bulbs used for decoration.

Recipe contest finalist: Linda Tarvin, Morgan Hill

4 cloves fresh garlic, minced
⅓ cup olive oil
⅔ cup white wine vinegar
⅓ cup dry red or white wine
2 tbsp. soy sauce
2 tbsp. honey
2 tbsp. chopped parsley
1 tbsp. salt
2 lbs. fresh mushrooms

Saute garlic in oil. Add vinegar, wine, soy sauce, honey, parsley and salt. Stir until mixture is well-blended and hot. Place mushrooms in heat-proof container with tightly fitting lid. Pour hot mixture over mushrooms; allow to marinate from 1 to 3 hours, or more, turning over several times. Save marinade for later use on more mushrooms or use it as a salad dressing.

ARTICHOKE HEARTS MARINATI

From nearby Castroville come the artichoke hearts for this popular Italian antipasto. Whole artichokes may also be steamed or boiled until tender, the marinade spooned over them and chilled for about 6 hours, then served cold.

1 9 oz. package frozen artichoke hearts
2 tbsp. lemon juice
2 tbsp. olive oil
¾ tsp. garlic salt
¼ tsp. oregano leaves
¼ tsp. chervil leaves
¼ tsp. tarragon leaves

Cook artichoke hearts following directions on package. Drain and put in small bowl. Combine remaining ingredients and pour over artichoke hearts. Chill at least 2 hours before serving.

ROSE EMMA'S EGGPLANT RELISH

Eggplant is a very versatile vegetable and it's at its best when flavored with garlic, onions and tomatoes.

Courtesy of: Rose Emma Pelliccione, Gilroy

3 cups eggplant, peeled and cut in ½-inch cubes
⅓ cup chopped green peppers
1 medium onion, minced
3 cloves garlic, pressed
⅓ cup oil
1 6 oz. can tomato paste
1 4 oz. can mushroom stems and pieces
½ cup pimiento-stuffed olives
¼ cup water
2 tbsp. red wine vinegar
1½ tsp. sugar
1 tsp. seasoned salt
½ tsp. oregano
¼ tsp. pepper

Put eggplant, green pepper, onion, garlic and oil in skillet. Cover and cook gently for ten minutes, stirring occasionally. Add tomato paste, mushrooms with liquid and remaining ingredients. Cover and simmer 30 minutes. Turn into covered dish; refrigerate overnight to blend flavors. Serve with crackers and chips. Makes about one quart. Also keeps well frozen.

CREAMY GARLIC HERB CHEESE

Creamy-rich and delightfully herbed, Boursin cheese is a favorite spread for crackers. Here's an easy homemade version that tries to capture a similiar flavor.

Recipe contest entry: Julie and Gary Crites, La Verne

2 8 oz. packages cream
  cheese
1 pint sour cream
½ cup butter
3 cloves fresh garlic,
  pressed
¼ cup snipped chives

Mix all ingredients in blender or food processor. Chill in refrigerator several hours. Warm to room temperature before serving with crackers or as a dip for fresh raw vegetables.

GOURMET ALLEY'S STUFFED MUSHROOMS

Rancher/Chef Jim Rubino shares his recipe for the stuffed mushrooms that were a hit at the Festival's Gourmet Alley. These mushrooms make great finger appetizers for company (but don't forget your family too). Prepare them the day before or at the last minute but be sure to make plenty for they'll quickly disappear.

Courtesy of: Jim Rubino, San Martin

20 fresh mushrooms
½ cup finely chopped fresh
  parsley
¼ cup (1½ oz.) freshly
  grated Parmesan cheese
4 cloves fresh garlic
2 tbsp. soft butter

Clean mushrooms and remove stems. Combine parsley, cheese, garlic and butter into a firm stuffing mixture. Place approximately 1 tsp. stuffing into each mushroom. Place mushrooms on a flat baking pan on rack 6 inches under a preheated broiler. Broil for 4 to 5 minutes until mushrooms are cooked *al dente* and still firm. Do not overcook.

T he main attraction was the cooking contest and it was a doozy. The winners were real winners.
Food and Wine Magazine

Vegetables, Salads and Dressings

"Wel loved he garleek, onyons and eek lekes," it was said in the *Canterbury Tales.* And still these pungent bulbs continue to be enjoyed for their satisfying aroma and the zesty flavor they impart. Vegetable dishes respond particularly well to the addition of garlic during preparation, whether they are steamed, baked, stir-fried or combined in such spectacular dishes as Gilroy Ratatouille or Hollister Vegetable Casserole. And when it comes to salads, what dressing is not improved by the addition of garlic? We know of none.

QUICK AND EASY RECIPE IDEAS

Perk up frozen spinach with garlic. Simply cook spinach in a little water until thawed, then add pressed fresh garlic cloves and butter. Heat just until done.

Cook green beans in wine for real flavor enhancement. Partially steam the beans, then cook in white wine, fresh minced garlic and butter.

Give Quiche Lorraine a sassy twist by adding fresh minced garlic to the filling.

Potatoes go from ordinary to extra-delicious when fried with minced fresh garlic cloves. Season with garlic salt and sprinkle with grated cheese.

When cooking vegetables, add some sliced fresh garlic cloves to the cooking water to impart subtle flavor.

Here's a basic formula for salad dressing: Combine three parts oil with one part vinegar or lemon juice. Season with salt, freshly ground pepper and one or more cloves of crushed fresh garlic. Shake well in a screw-top jar and let stand for a few hours to blend flavors. Remove garlic before serving. Vary the basic dressing by adding other herbs and spices.

For discreet garlic flavor in your salad, rub halved cloves of fresh garlic on a crust of bread (called a *chapon,* in French), then wipe the salad bowl with the bread before adding greens.

GARLICKY MUSHROOMS SUPREME

This great mushroom dish can substitute for one of the vegetables at your next dinner party.   *Recipe contest entry: Carrie Cohen, Woodland Hills*

1 lb. sliced mushrooms
4 tbsp. olive oil
7 cloves fresh garlic, sliced
3 tbsp. chopped parsley
Salt and pepper to taste

Saute mushrooms in olive oil, covered, about 15 minutes. Uncover; add garlic, parsley, salt and pepper. Simmer until liquid evaporates. Do not let garlic brown. Serve and enjoy.

ALI BABA'S CARROTS

This cold vegetable side dish is perfect with a summer meal of barbecued meat, beans and potato salad. It can be made a day or two ahead, which even improves its flavor.

Recipe contest entry: Phyllis Gaddis, Venice

2 lbs. carrots
Boiling water
6 tbsp. water or chicken broth
6 tbsp. olive oil
7 cloves fresh garlic
Salt and pepper
3 tbsp. tarragon or white wine vinegar
½ tsp. dill weed
¼ tsp. cayenne
¼ tsp. paprika
¼ tsp. cumin
2 tbsp. chopped parsley

Peel carrots and cut into 2-inch pieces. Blanch in boiling water for one minute, then plunge into bowl of cold water. After two minutes, remove from cold water and drain. Meanwhile, in saucepan, heat water or chicken broth with olive oil, two whole cloves garlic, and salt and pepper to taste. Bring to a boil, then add carrots. Lower heat and simmer until tender but firm. Drain carrots, reserving liquid and whole cloves garlic. In a glass or plastic bowl large enough to hold carrots, mix marinade by combining vinegar, dill weed, cayenne, paprika, cumin, 5 garlic cloves (minced) and salt and pepper to taste. Add whole cloves garlic and reserved liquid. Cover and chill in refrigerator at least 6 hours (or as long as a day or two). To serve, drain carrots from marinade and place in dish. Sprinkle with chopped parsley. Makes 6 servings.

BASQUE-STYLE EGGPLANT CASSEROLE

Basques, people from northern Spain and southwestern France, are noted for serving foods with robust flavor. They love their garlic, too!

6 tbsp. oil
1 onion, sliced into rings
2 green peppers, cut into strips
5 large mushrooms, sliced
1 celery stalk, sliced diagonally
5 cloves fresh garlic, minced
6 tomatoes, peeled and diced
Salt to taste
1 tbsp. fines herbes
1 large eggplant
2 eggs, beaten with 1 tbsp. water and pinch of salt
½ cup freshly grated Parmesan cheese
1 cup grated Swiss cheese

Heat 3 tbsp. oil in large skillet; add onion, green peppers, mushrooms, celery and garlic. Saute until tender. Add tomatoes. Bring to a boil. Add salt and fines herbes. Turn heat to low and simmer sauce for 30 minutes. Peel eggplant and slice into ½-inch slices. Dip in egg mixture and fry eggplant in skillet with remaining oil until tender. Arrange eggplant slices in large baking dish. Sprinkle with Parmesan cheese. Pour tomato sauce over the top and sprinkle with Swiss cheese. Heat in 350°F oven until cheese is melted. Makes 4 servings.

CHINA CAMP STIR-FRIED VEGETABLES

Without fresh garlic, stir-fry vegetables might be good but not great. This combination is the greatest!

2 tbsp. oil
4 cloves fresh garlic
2 lbs. vegetables cut into ½-inch diagonal slices (asparagus, broccoli, green beans, etc.)
1 8 oz. can water chestnuts, drained and sliced
2 tbsp. soy sauce
Salt and pepper to taste
¼ cup toasted nuts, if desired (peanuts, almonds, cashews, etc.)

Heat in oil in large skillet or wok. Smash garlic by whacking cloves with butt end of a knife handle. Remove peel. Add garlic to oil. When garlic begins to give off aroma, remove and discard. Add vegetables and stir-fry over high heat until crisp-tender. Add water chestnuts, soy sauce, salt and pepper. Stir-fry another minute to heat through. Sprinkle with nuts and serve at once. Makes 4 to 6 servings.

SNOW PEAS CANTON

The Chinese have had a strong influence on California's history as well as its cuisine, and who knows better than the Chinese how to combine vegetables and garlic into mouth-watering dishes like this one!

1 tbsp. peanut oil
4 to 5 cloves fresh garlic, minced
½ lb. Chinese pea pods, ends trimmed, strings removed
1 5 oz. can sliced bamboo shoots, drained
1 8 oz. can water chestnuts, drained and sliced
¼ cup canned or fresh chicken broth
2 tsp. soy sauce
1 tsp. cornstarch
2 tsp. water

Heat oil in a large skillet or wok. Saute garlic until light brown. Add peas, bamboo shoots and water chestnuts. Stir-fry one minute. Add chicken broth and soy sauce. Cover and cook another minute. Combine cornstarch and water. Stir into skillet. Cook over high heat until sauce thickens and appears glossy, about one minute. Makes 4 servings.

GREEK BEANS

The Greeks also know how to season food well with garlic. This dish is particularly easy to prepare, but good enough for company!

Recipe contest entry: Barbara Flory, South Laguna

1 lb. fresh green beans
1 cup tomato juice
¼ cup olive oil
3 cloves fresh garlic, pressed
3 tomatoes, cut in quarters
1 chopped onion
½ cup chopped parsley
½ tsp. crushed oregano leaves
½ tsp. paprika
1 tsp. garlic salt
Salt and pepper to taste

Cut beans into thirds. Cook in tomato juice until tender. Meanwhile, in olive oil, saute garlic, tomatoes, onion, parsley and oregano until tender but still crisp. When beans are tender, add sauted ingredients, paprika, garlic salt and salt and pepper to taste. Simmer 5 more minutes, then serve.

HOLLISTER VEGETABLE CASSEROLE

A finalist in the Garlic Recipe Contest and Cook-off, Lena says this entry is a favorite with her family and some of the Gavilan College staff where she is Cafeteria Manager. "This dish is particularly good for vegetarians," says Lena. It would also be a good choice as a side dish to serve with barbecued meats.

Recipe contest finalist: Lena Lico, Hollister

6 zucchini, sliced
6 potatoes, peeled and sliced
3 bell peppers, cut in strips
2 large onions, sliced
1 large eggplant, sliced
½ cup Romano or Parmesan Cheese
Salt and pepper to taste
5 cloves fresh garlic, pressed
1 tsp. oregano
8 large tomatoes, sliced, or 2 lbs. canned tomatoes, broken up
½ cup oil

Place layers of vegetables in greased baking pan alternating with 4 tbsp. grated cheese, salt and pepper. Combine garlic and oregano with tomatoes. Top the casserole with tomatoes and 4 tbsp. cheese. Drizzle oil over top. Cover and bake at 350° for 1½ hours. Uncover and bake at 375°F for another 1½ hours.

ARTICHOKE AND CARROT FRITTATA

This vegetable frittata is excellent served as an evening main course or for a brunch. It could be topped with a white sauce and garnished with sliced ripe olives or served on bread as a sandwich filling.

Recipe contest entry: Fanny Cimoli, San Jose

2 cups sliced or chopped cooked artichoke hearts
8 eggs, beaten
1 cup grated cheese (Italian or American)
1 cup grated carrot
½ cup finely chopped parsley
½ cup chopped onion
⅛ cup chopped celery
5 cloves fresh garlic, minced
1 tbsp. catsup
1 tsp. salt
¼ tsp. pepper
Garlic salt to taste

Combine all ingredients together and blend well. Pour into large oblong baking dish (9x11), lightly greased. Bake until golden brown for 20 to 30 minutes at 300°F. Do not overbake, as it may become dry. Cut into squares and serve.

GARLIC BUTTER CRUMB TOMATOES

Karen Christopher, wife of Gilroy garlic grower and shipper Don Christopher says, "I'm not a person who enjoys long hours in the kitchen, but I always serve dishes laced with fresh garlic. This recipe for crumb topped tomatoes makes up fast and easy." They are attractive to serve and a happy blend of flavors which make them a good choice for the second vegetable.   *Courtesy of: Karen Christopher, Gilroy*

4 fresh tomatoes
½ cup seasoned dressing mix, crushed into crumbs
4 tbsp. melted butter
2 large cloves fresh garlic, minced
½ tsp. basil
Salt and pepper to taste
Fresh minced garlic

Cut tomatoes into halves. Moisten crumbs with mixture of butter, garlic, basil and seasonings. Place crumb mixture on tomato halves and broil in preheated broiler 10 inches from heat source until browned and heated. Garnish with minced parsley and serve.

EGGPLANT PARMIGIANA

This famous Italian dish takes full advantage of the wonderful flavor combination of garlic, tomatoes and Parmesan cheese.

2 medium eggplant
Oil for frying
2 cups canned tomatoes
1 6 oz. can tomato paste
¾ tsp. garlic powder
1½ tsp. seasoned salt
1/8 tsp. black pepper
1 tbsp. parsley flakes
1 bay leaf
½ cup grated Parmesan cheese
2 cups soft bread crumbs
½ lb. sliced Mozzarella cheese

Peel eggplant and cut into ½-inch slices. Saute in oil 5 minutes or until tender and lightly browned. Remove and keep warm. In skillet combine tomatoes, tomato paste, garlic powder, seasoned salt, pepper, parsley flakes and bay leaf. Cover and simmer 15 minutes. Remove bay leaf; add Parmesan cheese and bread crumbs, mixing well. Place a layer of eggplant in buttered, shallow 2-quart baking dish. Cover with half the tomato sauce then with half the Mozzarella cheese. Repeat layers. Bake in 350°F oven 20 minutes or until cheese melts and is lightly browned. Serve at once. You will find this dish excellent for Lent. Makes 5 to 6 servings.

VAL AND ELSIE'S JULIENNE BEANS

Val Filice, garlic grower and head chef of Gourmet Alley, and his wife Elsie even glamorize canned green beans when cooking at home!

Courtesy of: Val and Elsie Filice, Gilroy

4 cloves fresh garlic, crushed
1 bacon strip, cut crosswise into ¼ inch strips
4 tbsp. olive oil
3 cans (1 lb. each) julienne-style green beans
¼ cup liquid reserved after draining beans
1 tsp. dry oregano
1 tsp. dry basil (or fresh)
Salt and pepper to taste

Saute garlic and bacon in olive oil until garlic turns amber in color. Remove pan from heat and add beans, liquid, herbs, and salt and pepper and cook over medium heat until beans are warmed through.

ZESTY ZUCCHINI SAUTE

A quick and tasty way to serve zucchini, this dish goes well with any meat.

4 medium-sized zucchini
2 tsp. seasoned salt
2 tsp. parsley flakes
1 tsp. instant minced onion
½ tsp. ground oregano
¼ tsp. garlic powder
¼ tsp. pepper
¼ cup olive oil

Wash zucchini but do not peel. Slice in rounds about ¼ inch thick. Mix together remaining ingredients except olive oil. Sprinkle over zucchini and toss until seasoning is well distributed. Heat oil in skillet; add zucchini and saute until browned on both sides, about 10 minutes. Drain on absorbent paper. Makes 4 servings.

CAULIFLOWER WITH GARLIC OIL

This unusual treatment gives cauliflower a delightfully different flavor.

1 head cauliflower or broccoli
1 cup olive oil
½ tsp. salt
4 cloves fresh garlic, minced
2 tbsp. chopped parsley
3 hard-cooked eggs, chopped

Separate cauliflower into florets and steam in a small amount of water or in steamer basket until crisp-tender. Drain and set aside in warmed serving dish. Heat oil and salt in small pan and cook garlic and parsley until garlic is lightly browned. Pour oil mixture over cauliflower and garnish with chopped egg. Makes 4 servings.

STUFFED ARTICHOKES CASTROVILLE

The garlic and Parmesan cheese, classic flavor mates, make these stuffed artichokes a very special dish and one very popular, not only in Gilroy, but throughout the West.

Recipe contest entry: Nikki DeDominic, Guerneville

6 or 8 small artichokes
½ cup bread crumbs
½ cup grated Parmesan cheese
5 cloves fresh garlic
2 tbsp. parsley
Salt and pepper to taste
Olive oil

Clean outer leaves of artichokes and cut the tops and bottoms so they are flat. Scoop out choke, if desired. Mix bread crumbs, cheese, 3 cloves of garlic (minced), parsley, salt and pepper. Spread the leaves of artichokes and fill in every leaf with the bread mixture, including the center of the artichoke. In a low saucepan large enough to hold the artichokes, heat 1 tablespoon of oil and saute remaining 2 cloves of garlic (minced) until the garlic is slightly brown. Stand artichokes in the pan and fill pan with water to about 1 inch deep. (Water level depends on the size of the artichokes—do not allow water to reach bread crumb stuffing). Cover pan with aluminum foil to allow artichokes to steam. Cook until tender. If water evaporates before artichokes are ready, add more water.

CAPERED CARROTS AND ZUCCHINI

Two ordinary vegetables become special when sauteed with garlic and rosemary. Capers add an elegant touch and a spicy flavor.

Recipe contest entry: Angie Herrera, Norwalk

5 medium-sized carrots
3 small zucchini
2 tablespoons butter
3 cloves fresh garlic, minced
Pinch rosemary
Salt and pepper
Water
1 tbsp. capers

Slice carrots and zucchini about ¼ inch thick. Melt butter in a frying pan over medium heat; lightly saute garlic, then stir in carrots and cook 2 minutes. Stir in zucchini, rosemary, salt and pepper to taste. Stir until zucchini is heated through, then add 1 or 2 tablespoons water and cover pan. Cook over medium heat until carrots are barely fork tender, shaking pan and stirring occasionally. Don't overcook. Stir in capers and serve.

ZUCCHINI ALLA PELLICCIONE

Served as a cold side dish or salad, this minty marinated zucchini dish from a Gourmet Alley chef is an unusual accompaniment for almost any meal.

Courtesy of: Paul Pelliccione, Gilroy

7 to 8 zucchini (not over 2½-inch diameter)
Salt
2 cups flour
2 cups vegetable oil
3 cups dry bread crumbs
30 fresh garlic slices (6 to 8 cloves)
30 fresh mint leaves
Wine vinegar

Wash zucchini and trim ends. Slice uniformly to ³/₁₆-inch thickness. Arrange one layer in colander and sprinkle with salt. Continue with layers, sprinkling each with salt until all slices have been used. Let stand for 1 hour. Roll slices in flour and set aside. Heat oil to 300°F in large skillet. Fry slices on both sides until they barely begin to brown. Set aside on cookie sheet to cool completely. Place layer of sliced zucchini in large bowl. Sprinkle generously with bread crumbs. Arrange some of the garlic slices and mint leaves over the crumbs. Sprinkle generously with wine vinegar. Continue to layer zucchini and other ingredients in this order until all ingredients are used. Cover bowl and refrigerate.

TOMATOES A LA CLARE

"Delicious and pretty" says the woman who entered this recipe in The Great Garlic Recipe Contest. We have to agree.

Recipe contest entry: Clara M. Lutz, Redondo Beach

6 medium to large
tomatoes, sliced
3 cloves fresh garlic,
minced
1 bunch green onions,
chopped fine (include
some green tops)
⅓ cup finely chopped
parsley
½ tsp. salt
Coarse black pepper to
taste
⅓ cup corn oil
¼ cup brown cider vinegar
1 tbsp. Dijon mustard

Arrange tomatoes in a shallow dish or platter. Mix garlic, onions, parsley, salt and pepper; sprinkle over tomatoes. Cover with plastic wrap and refrigerate for 3 to 4 hours. Prepare dressing by combining oil, vinegar and mustard. At serving time, shake well and pour over tomatoes.

GILROY RATATOUILLE

Enhanced by sausage and cheese, this ratatouille makes a complete meal. For vegetarians, just omit the sausage.

Recipe contest entry: Mrs. Gene Stecyk, Los Angeles

3 cloves fresh garlic,
minced
2 thinly sliced onions
⅓ cup olive oil
1 green pepper, cut into
thin rounds
2 medium eggplant, diced,
unpeeled
2 medium zucchini, sliced
¼ inch thick
1 20 oz. can whole Italian
tomatoes
1½ tsp. basil
1½ tsp. parsley
1½ tsp. salt
Fresh ground pepper to
taste
1½ lbs. sliced Italian sausage
½ lb. whole mushrooms
1 cup grated Swiss cheese

Saute garlic and onions in oil until soft. Add green pepper, eggplant, and zucchini and cook five minutes over medium heat, tossing well. Add tomatoes with liquid and seasonings. Simmer uncovered 15 minutes, then cover and simmer 15 minutes more. Meanwhile, cook sausage in frying pan until done and drain well. Add mushrooms to vegetables during last 10 minutes of cooking time. Add sausage to vegetables. Sprinkle with grated cheese. Cover and simmer until cheese melts. Makes 8 servings.

VEGETABLES VERACRUZ

Inspired by the classic Mexican sauce for red snapper, this vegetable dish has a flavor all its own.

Recipe contest entry: Norman Simmons, Los Angeles

1 whole bulb fresh garlic
1 medium eggplant
  (approx. 1½ lbs.)
2 small zucchini
1½ tsp. salt
½ tsp. ascorbic acid (or fruit canning mix)
1 medium onion
¼ cup olive oil
2 tbsp. butter
1 tsp. oregano
1 tsp. sweet basil
¼ tsp. pepper
1 28 oz. can firm whole peeled tomatoes
1 tsp. cornstarch mixed with 1 tbsp. water

Separate the garlic cloves and remove skins. Peel and cut eggplant into ¾-inch cubes. Cut zucchini into ¾-inch rounds and then into quarters. Place zucchini and eggplant in a bowl and cover with water in which 1 tsp. salt and the ascorbic acid have been dissolved. Weight down and let stand while preparing remaining ingredients. Cut onion in half, then quarters and slice thinly. Reserve four garlic cloves and gently saute the remainder with onions in oil and butter on low heat for 10 minutes. Add oregano, basil, ½ tsp. salt, pepper and the drained liquid from the tomatoes. Reduce heat to simmer. Seed the drained tomatoes, cut them into ¾-inch pieces, and set aside. Steam zucchini and eggplant for ten minutes. When done, add to the onion and garlic mixture along with the tomatoes. Add reserved garlic cloves which have been minced fine. Raise heat and add the cornstarch in water, stirring until thickened and glazed. Simmer five minutes more and remove. *Do not overcook.* Let stand to blend flavors. This is delicious served hot or cold, and even better the next day. Makes 6 servings.

GREEN BEANS ASADOOR

There must be a thousand ways to serve green beans. This one has a wonderful Italian flavor.   *Recipe contest entry: Virginia Asadoor, Pasadena*

1 cup chopped onions
4 cloves fresh garlic
4 oz. butter or margarine
4 tbsp. tomato sauce
1 tsp. sweet basil
1 lb. fresh green beans, strings and ends removed.

Saute onions and garlic in butter; add tomato sauce and basil. Place green beans over onions and garlic; cover and simmer until cooked (approximately 15 to 20 minutes).

DILLED GREEN BEANS

It is always nice to have something homemade on the shelf to bring out to complete a party meal, sharpen your family's appetite or take as a house gift next time you visit friends. These dill- and garlic-flavored green beans would be welcome anytime.

2 lbs. green beans (young and tender)
1 tsp. powdered alum
1 gallon water
4 tsp. dill seed
2 tsp. mustard seed
1 tsp. crushed red pepper
1/2 tsp. dehydrated minced garlic
2 cups water
2 cups vinegar
1/4 cup salt

Wash beans and trim ends; place in stone crock or glass container. Dissolve alum in the 1 gallon water; pour over beans and let stand 24 hours. Drain and wash. Put beans in saucepan and add about 1 cup water. Cover and boil 5 minutes, then drain. Pack beans lengthwise into 4 sterilized canning jars. To each jar add 1 tsp. dill seed, 1/2 tsp. mustard seed, 1/4 tsp. crushed red pepper and 1/8 tsp. dehydrated garlic. Combine remaining ingredients and bring to a boil. Pour over beans, leaving 1/4-inch head space. Seal at once. Makes 4 jars beans.

THE GUBSERS' GREEN BEAN AND GARLIC FRITTATA

Joseph Gubser's father began growing garlic in Gilroy in the 1920s and to put it in Joe's words, "I grew up with the industry." This grower/shipper and his wife, Doris have contributed this unusual and tasty treatment for beans. It can be served as a cold vegetable dish or as an hors d'oeuvre.   *Courtesy of: Joseph and Doris Gubser, Gilroy*

1 green pepper, chopped
1 small onion, chopped
¼ cup plus 3 tbsp. olive oil
3 lbs. canned green beans, drained
¾ cup bread crumbs
½ cup grated Parmesan cheese plus additional cheese for topping
¼ cup sherry
3 eggs, beaten
3 large cloves fresh garlic, minced
1 tbsp. Italian seasoning
¼ tsp. salt
⅛ tsp. pepper
Paprika

Saute pepper and onion in 3 tbsp. olive oil. Combine with beans and all other ingredients (except paprika and cheese reserved for topping) into buttered (2 qt.) baking dish. Sprinkle with additional grated Parmesan and paprika. Bake in 325°F oven 40 minutes. Serve cold as a vegetable dish or as an hors d'oeuvre. Makes 10 to 12 servings.

BAKED GARLIC POTATOES

The goodness of garlic and the popular appeal of potatoes make this dish a winning combination. Small unpeeled potatoes are baked whole in a casserole and drizzled with garlic-flavored oil.

1 lb. small white potatoes (about 1½ inches in diameter)
4 cloves fresh garlic, minced
4 tbsp. olive oil
¼ cup chopped parsley
2 tsp. coarse salt
¼ tsp. freshly ground pepper
Butter or margarine

Wash and dry potatoes; arrange in a casserole in two layers. Combine garlic, oil, parsley, salt and pepper. Pour over potatoes and toss to coat with oil mixture. Cover and bake in a 450°F oven for 20 minutes. Turn potatoes to recoat in oil, then bake another 25 minutes. Cut potatoes open and squeeze ends to fluff them up. Serve with butter or margarine. Makes 6 servings.

LIGHT 'N' LOVELY EGGPLANT CASSEROLE

A different kind of eggplant dish, this recipe requires no cheese and no preliminary frying of the eggplant. It's great for controlled fat diets.   *Recipe contest entry: Joseph Noury, Sunnyvale*

4 large eggplant
3 large onions, diced
1 cup diced celery
5 cloves fresh garlic, minced
2 lbs. ground chuck
2 16 oz. cans tomatoes
1 6 oz. can tomato paste
1½ tsp. allspice

Cut eggplant in slices about ⅜ inch thick. Salt each slice and place in colander to drain. Combine onion, celery, garlic and ground meat in large pan. Brown all together, drain off fat and let cool. Crush tomatoes and combine with tomato paste and allspice. Bring to a slow boil for 15 minutes and then simmer for ½ hour. Let cool before using. Rinse off eggplant. Cover the bottom of a 10x13x2 baking pan with 1 cup tomato sauce mixture. Layer pan with eggplant, meat, and tomato mixture. You should be able to make three layers. Add meat and sauce on top layer. Cover with foil and bake at 350°F for ½ hour. Reduce heat to 300°F for ½ hour; remove foil and bake another 15 minutes. Serve over steamed rice.

QUEEN'S BEANS

This easy-to-fix vegetable dish can be a hearty meal-in-one with the addition of ham, ham hocks or hamburger.

Recipe contest entry: Mrs. Gil (Queen) Murphy, San Diego

1 cup small white beans
7 cups cold water
1 tsp. salt
¼ tsp. paprika
2 large onions, quartered
½ cup tomato sauce
10 large cloves fresh garlic, halved
½ cup parsley sprigs
¼ cup olive oil

Cook beans in water for 1 hour. Add salt, paprika and onions. Cover and cook 1 more hour. Add tomato sauce, garlic, parsley and olive oil. Cook 30 minutes longer. Serve with lemon juice.

CAESAR SALAD CALIFORNIA STYLE

In this version of Caesar Salad, it is important to prepare garlic-flavored oil several days ahead. Combine 1 cup olive oil with 1 cup sunflower oil and 7 cloves crushed, fresh garlic. Refrigerate for a few days, then strain. Now you're ready to fix the salad.

Recipe contest entry: Barbara Goldman, Granada Hills

1 loaf white bread, cut into small cubes
1 tsp. granulated garlic or garlic powder
Salt
12 to 14 oz. garlic-flavored oil (see recipe above)
1 clove fresh garlic
3 large heads romaine lettuce, torn into bite-sized pieces
Juice of 2 lemons
¾ cup Parmesan cheese
2 tsp. Worcestershire sauce
¾ tsp. pepper
5 eggs (at room temperature) coddled for 1½ minutes

Prepare croutons by placing cubed bread in deep roaster or baking dish. Sprinkle with granulated onion and garlic and ⅛ tsp. salt. Pour 6 oz. garlic-flavored oil over as evenly as possible. Bake at 225°F oven for 1 hour or until done. Turn every 15 minutes. Before preparing salad, rub large salad bowl with fresh garlic. Then add lettuce and toss with 10 oz. garlic-flavored oil to coat each leaf. Add lemon juice and toss again. Add cheese, Worcestershire and ¾ tsp. salt and pepper and 2 cups croutons. (Freeze remaining croutons for later use.) Toss salad thoroughly, but carefully. Then add eggs, toss gently and serve immediately.

JEANNE'S LOW-FAT CREAMY GARLIC DRESSING

This original low-calorie recipe is equally good as a dip or dolloped on crisp hearts of lettuce.

Recipe contest entry: Jeanne Marks, Aptos

4 large cloves fresh garlic
8 oz. plain low-fat yogurt
1 cup low-fat mayonnaise
¼ cup imitation bacon bits
½ tsp. prepared mustard

Put garlic through press or mince fine. Combine with remaining ingredients and serve as a dip or salad dressing.

GARLIC GREEN BEAN SALAD

A versatile, green bean dish that can be served as a side dish or combined with shredded iceberg lettuce for a delicious, crispy and satisfying salad.   *Recipe contest entry: Sylvia V. Biewener, Burbank*

2 lbs. fresh green beans
4 large cloves fresh garlic
1½ tsp. salt
½ cup oil
½ cup cider vinegar
¼ cup minced green onions
   (use some green tops)
1 small can chopped green chile peppers

Cut beans in 2-inch lengths. Boil until tender-crisp and drain. Peel garlic and mash with salt. Add oil, vinegar, onions and chiles. Pour over beans while hot. Toss gently. Refrigerate. Makes 6 to 8 servings.

GREEN GODDESS DRESSING

The original Green Goddess dressing was created by the chef of the Palace Hotel in San Francisco for a noted star in the days of the silent films. Without the garlic from Gilroy it would not be such a distinctive concoction! For a really new taste, top shrimp-filled papaya halves with Green Goddess dressing for lunch or a light supper.

1 2 oz. can anchovy fillets
3 cups mayonnaise
¼ cup wine vinegar
1 tbsp. chives
1 tbsp. minced green onion
1 tbsp. parsley flakes
1 tbsp. tarragon leaves
¼ tsp. garlic powder
⅛ tsp. onion powder
   Dash MSG (optional)

Mash anchovies. Add remaining ingredients; mix well. Let stand 30 minutes or longer for flavors to blend. Serve with salad greens. You may toss chicken, shrimp or crab meat with the greens. Makes about 3½ cups.

The festival was one of those happy bits of Americana when the whole town turns out.
MARJORIE RICE
Copley News Service

TART 'N' TANGY ITALIAN DRESSING

It is so simple to make a truly appealing Italian salad dressing and it can be done as close as one hour before serving time. Use as a marinade, too, for steaks and chops.

1 cup olive oil
½ cup wine vinegar
1 tsp. instant minced onion
1 tsp. seasoned salt
¾ tsp. garlic powder
½ tsp. chives
½ tsp. parsley flakes
½ tsp. sugar
¼ tsp. dry mustard
¼ tsp. oregano
1/8 tsp. white pepper
   Dash cayenne or red
   pepper

Combine all ingredients in jar; cover and shake vigorously. Chill 1 hour for flavors to blend. Shake well before serving. Makes 1½ cups.

ITALIAN SWEET-SOUR DRESSING

Italians are full of surprises and the sweet-sour flavor captured in this dressing is certainly different. It's especially good over crisp chunks of iceberg lettuce.

1 cup vegetable oil
⅔ cup red wine vinegar
4 tbsp. sugar
1 tsp. salt
1 tsp. celery salt
1 tsp. coarsely ground
   pepper
1 tsp. dry mustard
1 tsp. Worcestershire sauce
½ tsp. bottled hot pepper
   sauce
3 cloves fresh garlic,
   minced

Thoroughly combine all ingredients in a jar or blender. Refrigerate. Makes 2 cups dressing.

GARLIC FRENCH DRESSING

This is a good basic dressing with subtle but pleasing garlic flavor. For variety add ¾ cup crumbled Roquefort cheese, a chopped hard-cooked egg, or 3 tablespoons chopped onion.

Recipe contest entry: Barbara Van Brunt Halop, Los Angeles

2¼ cups salad oil
1 cup mayonnaise
¾ cup wine or cider vinegar
8 cloves fresh garlic,
   pressed or minced
2 tsp. salt
1½ tsp. sugar
1½ tsp. paprika
1½ tsp. dry mustard
1½ tsp. Worcestershire sauce
¾ tsp. coarse ground pepper
¼ tsp. garlic salt
¼ tsp. onion salt
¼ tsp. celery salt
¼ tsp. seasoned salt
¼ cup catsup or chili sauce
   for color

Combine all ingredients and blend well. Refrigerate in covered container approximately 24 hours before using.

KAREN'S FRESH PEARS WITH GARLIC ROQUEFORT DRESSING

The man of the house is of Danish ancestry and grows garlic and comice pears. What better combination to keep him content than Roquefort cheese and garlic dressing on fresh comice pears? A classic combination that makes a terrific salad.

Courtesy of: Karen Christopher, Gilroy

½ cup mayonnaise
1 tbsp. cream
1 tbsp. lemon juice
2 cloves fresh garlic,
   pressed
1½ oz. Roquefort or blue
   cheese, crumbled
8 fresh comice pears
   Lemon juice
8 lettuce leaves

Mix together mayonnaise, cream, 1 tbsp. lemon juice, garlic and cheese and chill at least 2 hours. Cut pears in half and remove seeds and skins. Sprinkle with additional lemon juice to prevent browning. Place on lettuce leaves for individual servings, spoon dressing, and serve. Makes 8 salads.

    This dressing is also delicious on most greens or can be used as a dip for fresh raw vegetables.

SPICY MARINATED SHRIMP FOR A CROWD

Shrimp take a tangy bath in a spicy oil and vinegar marinade. When drained and arranged in lettuce cups with tomato and cucumber garnish, these marinated beauties make elegant, individual salads.

8 to 10 small shrimp in shell
1½ cups dehydrated, sliced or chopped onion
1½ cups water
1 quart olive oil
1½ pints cider vinegar
1 pint capers with juice
¼ cup lemon juice
2 tbsp. sugar
2 tbsp. Worcestershire sauce
2 tsp. salt
¾ tsp. instant granulated garlic
Few drops hot pepper sauce

Cook shrimp, peel, devein and rinse well. Reconstitute the dehydrated onion in 1½ cups of water. Alternate layers of shrimp and reconstituted onions in large flat pan. Combine remaining ingredients and pour over both shrimp and onions. Cover and refrigerate overnight. Drain and serve in lettuce cups. Garnish with tomato and cucumber. Makes about 30 servings.

ROSIE'S BROCCOLI SALAD

Tart and tangy garlic marinade adds zip to steamed broccoli.

Recipe contest entry: Carla Johnson, Petaluma

2 bunches broccoli
¼ cup olive oil
3 to 4 cloves fresh garlic, pressed or minced
½ tsp. salt
¼ tsp. oregano
¼ cup wine vinegar

Cut off tough ends of broccoli and discard. Slice remaining stems and flowers into bite-sized pieces which should equal about 14 cups uncooked. Steam or boil broccoli until just tender. Drain and cool. Toss broccoli with olive oil, garlic, salt and oregano. Add vinegar and toss again. Refrigerate at least one hour to marinate before serving. This can be prepared the day prior to serving, and served chilled or at room temperature.

PARTY-PERFECT GARLIC DRESSING

When it's party time and you're planning a salad, try this flavorful combination. It makes a gallon of tangy dressing to perk up any fresh vegetable combination.

1⅓ tsp. curry powder
1⅓ tsp. dry mustard
2 tsp. cayenne
1 tbsp. dehydrated parsley
1 tbsp. dehydrated chives
1 tsp. instant granulated garlic
¼ cup salt
1 tbsp. white pepper
1 lemon rind, chopped
⅓ cup olive oil
1 cup white wine vinegar
2½ quarts salad oil
1¼ quarts cider vinegar

Moisten instant granulated garlic, parsley and chives with ¼ cup water. To this add curry, mustard, cayenne, salt, pepper and lemon rinds. While beating, first add olive oil, then vinegar. Chill well. Shake before serving. Makes about 1 gallon.

GEORGETTE'S FRENCH DRESSING

This is a low-calorie, low-salt salad dressing that is great on any mixed green salad. It was named after the late Georgette Smith, home economics teacher at Gavilan Junior College in Gilroy.

Courtesy of: Louis Bonesio, Jr., Gilroy

1 cup low-sodium tomato juice
1 cup red wine vinegar
1 cup polyunsaturated oil
¼ cup honey
3 to 4 cloves fresh garlic, minced
½ tsp. paprika
½ tsp. coarse pepper
¼ tsp. dry mustard
¼ tsp. curry powder

Combine all ingredients and beat with a rotary beater or shake in a tightly covered jar. Shake well before serving. A little grated Parmesan cheese as a garnish and some sourdough bread for a "backstop" is good.

SOUPS

An ancient Telugu (India) proverb states "Garlic is as good as ten mothers." Similarly, "Our doctor is a clove of garlic," an adage of the 17th century, implies that garlic is healthful and good for treating various ailments. The idea prevails today, and mothers around the world are still prescribing old-fashioned, garlic-laced soup, especially for the common cold. While the potential medicinal values of garlic have not yet been proven, there is no doubt about the flavor benefits to be derived by the addition of garlic, a little or a lot, to almost any soup. You'll find here wonderful recipes for everything from Gumbo and Gazpacho to Avocado, Cucumber and Potato Soups. And, of course, two first-rate versions of the classic "Garlic Soup."

"This is no fad. Garlic is chic now—finally." Don Christopher agreed with a smile. "The future is real rosy for garlic and also for Gilroy."

Los Angeles *Times*

THE CHRISTOPHERS' GARLIC SOUP

One of the organizers of the festival, garlic grower and shipper Don Christopher, devised this recipe for garlic soup after a trip to Mexico. He relates he made it a dozen times before he was satisfied that he had it right. Now it's one of his favorites. It's delicious when reheated too.

Courtesy of: Don Christopher, Gilroy

  6 beef flavored bouillon
     cubes
  8 cups boiling water
 14 large cloves fresh garlic
  2 tbsp. butter
  2 tbsp. minced parsley
  1 tbsp. flour
 ¼ tsp. freshly ground pepper
  6 raw egg yolks, beaten
  6 thin slices Monterey Jack
     cheese
  6 small slices French bread,
     toasted

In large bowl or saucepan, combine bouillon cubes and water, stirring until cubes are dissolved. Peel garlic and mince (can be done quickly in a blender or food processor). In heavy saucepan, over low heat, brown garlic lightly in butter with minced parsley stirring constantly so as not to burn. Add flour and stir until slightly browned. Add broth and pepper; simmer at least 30 minutes to 1 hour. Just before serving, slowly add egg yolks, stirring constantly. Place cheese on toasted bread and place 1 slice in each serving bowl. Ladle soup into bowl and place bowl under broiler just long enough to melt cheese. (This could also be done in the microwave oven). Serve at once. Makes 6 generous servings.

Community leaders
agreed that the time
had come for garlic
to come storming
out of the pantry
closet.
MIKE DUNNE
Sacramento *Bee*

CAULDITO DE AJOS   *Little Soup of Garlic*

This light, fresh tasting soup would be very satisfying served in mugs on a cold night. The combination of cilantro and lime with the garlic flavor is most interesting.

Recipe contest entry: Anne Copeland MacCallum, San Pedro

¼ cup peeled and chopped fresh garlic
¼ cup oil
Juice of 1 lime
6 cups chicken broth
Salt and pepper to taste
2 eggs
Grated rind of one lime
Cilantro (fresh coriander, also called Mexican parsley)

Saute garlic in oil until golden. Add with lime juice to chicken broth. Add salt and pepper and bring to a boil. Lower heat and continue to simmer for 15 to 20 minutes, or until the garlic taste permeates the soup. Meanwhile, blend eggs and grated lime rind in a bowl, adding a little salt and pepper. Add egg mixture to garlic soup a little at a time, stirring constantly. Turn up heat slightly, but do not allow soup to boil. Continue to cook about 5 minutes. Serve with chopped cilantro and sliced limes for garnish.

ITALIAN SAUSAGE SOUP

You can make a meal of this soup. Just serve with a green salad, plenty of crusty French bread and . . . red wine, perhaps.

1 lb. Italian sausage, cut in ½-inch slices
4 cloves fresh garlic, minced
2 large onions, chopped
1 16 oz. can Italian pear tomatoes
1½ quarts canned beef broth or prepared from bouillon cubes and water
1½ cups red wine (or water)
½ tsp. basil
½ tsp. thyme
3 tbsp. chopped parsley
1 medium-sized green pepper, chopped
2 medium-sized zucchini, sliced
3 cups uncooked *farfalle* (bow-tie noodles)
Parmesan cheese, grated

In a 5-quart kettle, brown sausage on medium heat. *Drain fat.* Add garlic and onions; cook until limp. Stir in and break up tomatoes. Add broth, wine, basil, thyme and parsley. Simmer uncovered for 30 minutes. Add vegetables and noodles. Cover and simmer 25 minutes more. Sprinkle each serving with Parmesan cheese. Makes 8 to 10 servings.

BULGARIAN CUCUMBER YOGURT SOUP

All over the world, Bulgarians are known for their good health and longevity, which are often attributed to their consumption of yogurt and garlic. This soup combines both in a delicious adaptation of a classic Bulgarian recipe.   *Recipe contest entry: Annegret Yonkow, Fairfax*

1 large cucumber
½ cup finely chopped walnuts
4 cloves fresh garlic, minced
3 tbsp. chopped parsley
2 tbsp. oil
1 tsp. dill weed
½ tsp. salt
2 cups European-style yogurt (without gelatin)
2 cups ice water
Ice

Peel cucumber and shred or chop very fine. Mix with all other ingredients except yogurt, water and ice. Cover and refrigerate for several hours to allow flavors to blend. At serving time add yogurt and water and a few pieces of ice.

COLD BEET AND CUCUMBER SOUP

Even "buttermilk haters" will like this luscious and low-calorie soup.
Recipe contest entry: Ruth Gordon, Carpinteria

1 lb. can julienne beets
1 8 oz. carton low-fat yogurt
1 quart buttermilk
4 large cloves fresh garlic
2 unpeeled cucumbers
4 green onions with stems
Handful fresh parsley
1 chicken bouillon cube, dissolved in ½ cup water
White or black pepper to taste

Drain beets, reserving juice, and set aside in a large bowl. In blender or food processor, combine beet juice, yogurt, buttermilk and garlic. (Depending on work bowl capacity you may have to do this in portions.) Pour over julienne beets. In same blender, coarsely chop cucumbers, onions and parsley, using chicken bouillon for the liquid. Add to beet mixture. Stir well and add pepper to taste. Refrigerate overnight in covered container. Serve very cold.

SPICY CALIFORNIA GUMBO

If you are not familiar with Creole cookery, you may not know that the term "to rope" refers to the stringy strands which okra exudes when it first starts to cook. You may also not be familiar with filé powder which is a very important ingredient. It is made from the ground young leaves of dried sassafras and used both to season and thicken soups and stews.   *Recipe contest entry: Jeani Cearlock, Morgan Hill*

¼ cup butter
½ lb. fresh okra
1 large onion, chopped
1½ large stalks celery, sliced
½ cup chopped green
  pepper
5 cloves fresh garlic,
  minced
2 to 3 tbsp. flour
1 jar medium-sized oysters,
  diced
2 cups chicken broth or
  bouillon
1½ large tomatoes, chopped
6 sprigs minced parsley
Pinch of thyme
Salt and pepper to taste
Tabasco sauce
Water
½ lb. diced ham
¾ lb. shrimp, shelled and
  deveined
Cooked rice
Filé powder

Melt butter in large pan. Add okra, onion, celery, green pepper and garlic and cook until okra ceases to "rope." Add flour and cook for 2 or 3 minutes. Add the liquid from the oysters, chicken broth, tomatoes, parsley, bay leaves, thyme, salt, pepper and Tabasco. Simmer about an hour (may need additional water). Add ham and simmer another 20 minutes. Add shrimp and oysters and simmer for 10 to 15 minutes. Remove bay leaves. To serve, put a scoop of rice in a soup bowl and add a generous amount of gumbo; sprinkle with a little filé powder and enjoy!

AVOCADO BISQUE

Everyone likes garlic as a flavoring in guacamole. It's equally good in this elegant avocado soup. *Recipe contest entry: Mrs. John Austad, San Diego*

2 bunches spinach, heated
  until just wilted but not
  cooked
2 medium-sized California
  avocados
4 to 5 cloves fresh garlic
1 cup half-and-half
1 cup chicken broth
1 tbsp. butter
1 tsp. salt

Place all ingredients in blender and blend 45 seconds until creamy smooth. Pour into a saucepan and cover. Heat on medium until puffs of steam are seen at top. *Do not allow to boil*, as avocados will become bitter. Serve immediately. Makes about 1 quart.

GREAT GAZPACHO

The Spanish cold soup, gazpacho, is a pleasing addition to brunch or lunch and a welcome first course for dinner on hot summer days.

Recipe contest entry: Connie Rogers, Gilroy

2 medium cucumbers, peeled and coarsely chopped
5 medium tomatoes, peeled and coarsely chopped
1 large onion, coarsely chopped
1 medium green pepper, seeded and coarsely chopped
2 tsp. chopped fresh garlic
4 cups French or Italian bread, trimmed of crusts and coarsely crumbled
4 cups cold water
¼ cup red wine vinegar
4 tsp. salt
¼ cup olive oil
1 tbsp. tomato paste

In large, deep bowl combine cucumbers, tomatoes, onion, green pepper and garlic; add crumbled bread and mix together thoroughly; then stir in water, vinegar and salt. Ladle about 2 cups of the mixture at a time into a blender and blend at high speed for 1 minute, or until it is a smooth puree. Pour puree into a bowl and, with a whisk, beat in olive oil and tomato paste. Cover bowl tightly and refrigerate for at least 2 hours or until thoroughly chilled. Just before serving, stir soup lightly to recombine it.

Garnishes
1 cup small homemade croutons
½ cup finely chopped onions
½ cup peeled and finely chopped cucumbers
½ cup finely chopped green peppers

Serve the garnishes in separate small bowls so that each diner may add his/her own according to preference.

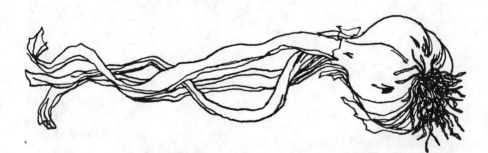

GAZPACHO FOR A CROWD

A big bowl of gazpacho surrounded by crushed ice to keep it well chilled, can be, pardon the pun, an "ice breaker" for any party. Guests can step up and help themselves, while the hostess prepares the next course.

16 lbs. tomatoes, diced
4 medium-sized cucumbers, diced
1 cup dehydrated green bell peppers
½ cup dehydrated chopped or minced onion
½ tsp. instant granulated garlic
1 quart soft bread crumbs
1 gallon water
2 tsp. crushed red pepper
¼ cup salt
2 tbsp. olive oil
3 cups vinegar
1 cup pimiento-stuffed green olives, chopped
¼ cup parsley flakes
¼ cup dehydrated celery granules

Combine tomatoes, cucumbers, green bell peppers, onion, garlic, bread crumbs and water. Bring to a boil. Cover and simmer 1 hour. Force through a sieve or food mill. Add pepper, salt, oil and vinegar. Mix well. Chill thoroughly. Serve with olives, parsley, and celery as toppings. Makes about 25 servings.

BLOODY MARY PARTY SOUP

Cocktails in the soup bowl? Why not! This spicy tomato soup is laced with vodka poured at the table from a bottle which has been frozen into a block of ice. Dramatic and lots of fun as a starter course for a brunch or light supper.

2½ cups minced onion
2 cups minced celery
1¼ cups peeled, seeded and minced cucumber
8 cloves fresh garlic, minced
2 tbsp. butter or margarine
4 cans (46 oz. each) tomato juice
1½ cups lemon juice
3 tbsp. sugar
½ tsp. Tabasco sauce
½ tsp. Worcestershire sauce
1 bottle (fifth) vodka
½ cup green onion, sliced

Saute onion, celery, cucumber and garlic in butter until soft. Add tomato juice, lemon juice, sugar, Tabasco and Worcestershire; simmer 7 to 8 minutes. Chill. Place vodka bottle in No. 10 can filled with water; freeze until ice is solid. Remove can but keep vodka surrounded in ice and wrapped in a towel. To serve: portion soup into serving bowl. Garnish with green onion. Add 1 oz. jigger of vodka (from bottle in ice block) per serving of soup at table. Make 24 servings (about 1 cup each).

MAMA'S POTATO SOUP

Don't let the homespun name of this spicy Mexican-style soup fool you. It's a great dish to serve company as well as your family.

Recipe contest entry: Edna H. Ramirez, Monterey Park

2 tbsp. oil
4 cloves fresh garlic, minced
1 cup finely chopped onion
3 medium-sized tomatoes, peeled and chopped
½ cup chopped green chiles
1 tbsp. flour
2 quarts hot chicken broth
2½ cups peeled raw potatoes, cut into small cubes
2 tsp. salt (or to taste)
1 tsp. black pepper
2 medium-sized carrots, peeled and thinly sliced
1 medium-sized zucchini, thinly sliced
2 cups Monterey Jack cheese, cut into small cubes

Heat oil in 3-quart saucepan and add garlic, onions, tomatoes and green chiles; saute for 3 minutes. Stir in flour and cook for 2 more minutes. Continue stirring as you pour in the hot broth. Add potatoes, salt and pepper. Cover pan and simmer over low heat for 20 minutes. Add carrots and zucchini and cook for 15 minutes longer or until potatoes are tender. Just before serving add the cubed cheese. Makes 4 to 6 servings.

Breads and Pasta

History recounts that the great pyramids of Egypt might not have been built without the nourishment of garlic and onions, which served as a mainstay to those who laid the cornerstones of ancient Egyptian architecture. Today garlic plays an equally important role in flavoring the many breads and pastas which are cornerstones of the diets of people throughout the world. Almost everyone has a special way of preparing the popular garlic bread. There are a number of variations, plus some tips from experts, included in this section, as well as a garlic croissant recipe which qualified as one of the ten Garlic Recipe Contest and Cook-off finalists. For pasta lovers there are recipes using linguine, spaghetti, fettuccine, tagliarini, capellini and vermicelli . . . . and all of them *delizioso!*

GARLIC BREAD

Fragrant garlic bread adds special delight to any meal. The main ingredients are garlic and butter or margarine, of course, but then it's cook's choice. The garlic used might be minced or pressed or the powdered variety from the spice shelf. Some like to add cheese or herbs or other secret ingredients. The bread may be baked, broiled or grilled. No matter how you like it, there's a garlic bread recipe for you. Recipes for garlic butter will be found in the Miscellaneous section of this book because they can also be used to season vegetables and other foods.

Quick Tips for Making Garlic Breads:

Take a tip from the French, who love their garlic. Rub toasted bread with a cut clove of garlic before buttering. The toast acts as a grater and leaves a layer of fresh garlic flavor on the bread.

Garlic toast can also be made by toasting bread and spreading with garlic puree or granulated garlic, then adding a sprinkle of grated bread crumbs and olive oil before browning in the oven.

Toasted English muffins or bagels can be good substitutes for French bread. They taste great with garlic butter.

For impromptu parties, keep garlic bread in the freezer. It will last for months if well-wrapped. When needed, just pop into the oven still frozen.

Use baked garlic cloves to spread on hot French bread. Bake whole bulbs with the skin left on in a little oil, either in a casserole or wrapped in foil in a moderate oven until soft. The cloves will pop right out of their skins and spread like butter.

MARY'S GARLIC BREAD

The Gilroy merchant who developed this recipe adds mayonnaise, cheese and herbs to her garlic butter mixture to achieve a fabulous flavor.   *Recipe contest entry: Mary Mozzone, Gilroy*

1 cup butter, softened
1 cup grated Parmesan
  cheese
½ cup mayonnaise
5 cloves fresh garlic,
  minced or pressed
3 tbsp. chopped fresh
  parsley
½ tsp. oregano
1 large loaf French bread,
  cut lengthwise

Mix all ingredients in bowl and spread on bread. Wrap in foil and bake at 375°F for 20 minutes. Unwrap and brown slightly under the broiler.

LEO'S SPECIAL GARLIC BREAD

Gourmet Alley chef Leo Goforth shares his version of garlic bread. You don't even have to mince or press fresh garlic to make Leo's specialty. Just cut cloves in half and rub over toasted French bread. It's fabulous!   *Courtesy of: Leo Goforth, Gilroy*

1 large loaf French bread,
  sweet or sourdough
4 large cloves garlic, peeled
  and cut in half
½ cup melted butter or
  margarine
2 tbsp. parsley, minced

Cut bread lengthwise and place on cookie sheet under broiler. Toast very lightly. Immediately rub cut end of garlic cloves over surface of bread. Brush on melted butter, sprinkle with minced parsley and return to oven to keep warm. Slice and arrange in serving basket.

CLASSIC GARLIC BREAD

Here's a classic bread treatment that makes perfect garlic bread every time. Just watch carefully to prevent burning!

Courtesy of: Karen Christopher, Gilroy

¾ cup melted butter
3 large cloves fresh garlic, minced or pressed
1 loaf fresh French bread (sweet)

Combine butter and garlic in pan over low heat until butter melts. Do not brown! Cut bread in half lengthwise. Cut diagonal slices 2 inches wide, but not all the way through the crust. Spoon garlic butter evenly on bread. Place bread halves on cookie sheet in preheated broiler about 9 inches from the source of heat. Broil until lightly browned. Watch carefully!

GRILLED GARLIC BREAD

When it's barbecue time, be sure to toss some garlic bread on the grill. Served piping hot, its zesty flavor adds a special touch to any outdoor meal.

1 loaf French bread
¾ tsp. garlic powder
½ cup softened butter or margarine

Slice bread but not through the bottom crust. Add garlic powder to butter and blend thoroughly. Spread between slices and over top of bread. Wrap in aluminum foil; seal edges. Heat on back of grill 45 minutes to 1 hour, depending on heat of coals. Serve hot. Makes 6 to 8 servings.

You could wash down the garlic sauce on garlic bread with garlic wine.

London *Daily Mail*

SPEEDY GARLIC CHEESE BREAD

No time to cook? Here's a garlic bread recipe that's a snap to prepare, relying on garlic powder for its mouth-watering appeal.

1 loaf French bread
¾ tsp. garlic powder
½ cup butter or margarine
1 cup Parmesan or sharp
   cheese, grated

Cut bread into 1-inch slices. Heat garlic powder and butter slowly until butter is melted. Brush each slice of bread on both sides with garlic butter and place on baking sheet. Sprinkle with cheese and bake in 425°F oven 10 minutes or until cheese melts. Serve hot. Makes 6 servings.

DILLY GARLIC ROLLS

Buttery, herbed rolls, piping hot from the grill are easy to make when you start with the ready-to-serve variety and add your own creative touches.

¼ cup softened butter
½ tsp. dill weed
¼ tsp. garlic powder
6 ready-to-serve pull apart
   rolls

Cream together butter, dill weed and garlic powder. Break rolls apart from the top and spread butter mixture between sections. Wrap in aluminum foil and place on grill and heat 10 minutes, turning once or twice.

CROISSANTS D'AIL   *Garlic Crescents*

Barbara Spellman, a home economics teacher, became a Garlic Contest finalist with this delightful recipe. Elegant and buttery, these lovely croissants get their appealing flavor from the creamy garlic butter that is mixed into the dough.

Recipe contest finalist: Barbara Spellman, Morgan Hill

Garlic Butter
   3 to 8 cloves fresh garlic
   1 quart boiling water
   4 tbsp. butter

Place unpeeled cloves of garlic in boiling water for 5 seconds. Drain, peel and rinse under cold water. Bring to a boil again for 30 seconds; drain and rinse. Pound into a smooth paste in a mortar or put through a garlic press. Soften butter and mix with the garlic paste. Set aside.

Croissant Dough
4 cups flour
6 tbsp. sugar
2 tsp. salt
2 oz. yeast, softened in ½
  cup warm water for about
  20 minutes
1 cup water or milk (plus or
  minus a little)
¾ cup butter

Sift together the flour, sugar and salt in a large mixing bowl. Add the softened yeast. Gradually add the water (milk) until the mixture forms a ball (you may need to vary this 1 cup of liquid more or less depending upon the moisture level of the flour.) Continue kneading in the bowl or on a lightly floured pastry cloth until a smooth, elastic dough is formed. Place about ⅓ of the dough back in the bowl, and add the garlic butter to it. When this is mixed into the dough, add the remaining ⅔ of the dough. Mix thoroughly. On a lightly floured cloth, roll the dough into a rectangle about ⅜ inch thick. Place ¾ cup butter (soft enough to spread) in the center of the dough. Bring each side up and over the butter. Seal the center and ends of the dough. Fold the dough into thirds; turn and roll to the size of the original rectangle. Repeat this process two more times. Fold the dough into thirds. Allow the dough to rise at room temperature until double. Place on a baking sheet and refrigerate 45 minutes to one hour, until dough is chilled. Remove from the refrigerator and roll into a rectangle about 10 inches by 20 inches. Cut into 10 rectangles about 4 inches by 5 inches. Cut each of these rectangles in half diagonally. Roll each piece of dough, beginning at the wide end; curve to crescent shape; place on an ungreased baking sheet and allow to rise until doubled in size (about 2 hours.) Paint with egg mixed with a small amount of water and bake in 400°F oven for 10 to 15 minutes, depending upon desired browness. *Optional:* Before rolling dough into crescent shape, sprinkle with freshly chopped parsley mixed with Parmesan cheese.

BUSY DAY GARLIC CASSEROLE BREAD

If baking bread seems like a chore, try this easy casserole bread, rich with the flavor of garlic and oregano.

Recipe contest entry: Dorothy Pankratz, Santa Clara

1 package dry yeast
1 cup cottage cheese, heated
4 cloves fresh garlic, pressed
1 unbeaten egg
1 tbsp. oil
1 tbsp. oregano
2 tsp. sugar
1 tsp. seasoned salt
¼ tsp. baking soda
2½ cups flour

Soften yeast in ¼ cup water. Combine in large mixing bowl with cottage cheese, garlic, egg, oil, oregano, sugar, salt, and soda. Add flour and blend well. Let rise until double. Stir down and turn into a greased casserole. Let rise 30 minutes. Bake for 40 minutes at 350°F.

EGGPLANT PASTA FANTASTICO

Eggplant and herbs, gently simmered, make a richly satisfying sauce for pasta. An extra sprinkling of Parmesan cheese adds zip.

Recipe contest entry: Leatrice Resnick, Los Angeles

½ cup olive oil
8 fresh garlic cloves, slivered
2 tbsp. minced onion
1 medium eggplant
1 tbsp. parsley flakes
1 tbsp. oregano flakes
1 tsp. basil
1 tsp. salt
½ tsp. ground pepper
½ to 1 cup water
Juice of ½ lemon
8 oz. spaghetti or linguine
½ cup pasta liquid
1 tbsp. grated Parmesan cheese plus additional cheese, if desired

In large skillet, heat olive oil. Add garlic and onion and slowly saute until lightly browned. While garlic is cooking, peel and dice eggplant into ½-inch cubes. Add eggplant, parsley, oregano, basil, salt and pepper to garlic mixture. Stir all ingredients well. Cover and cook over medium-low heat for 30 minutes, stirring occasionally. Add ½ cup water and lemon juice. Stir and continue cooking until eggplant is soft, adding more water as needed if mixture gets dry. (Mixture should be very moist.) Cook pasta *al dente* (just until tender; do not overcook). Drain pasta, reserve ½ cup liquid. Add pasta and liquid to eggplant mixture. Add Parmesan cheese. Toss well and heat through for 1 minute. Serve immediately with additional cheese, if desired. Makes 2 servings.

GARLIC IN THE STRAW AND HAY

The "straw" and "hay" refer to the white and green linguine that are combined to make this unique and colorful pasta presentation. Laced with sliced, fresh mushrooms and minced prosciutto and topped with a creamy cheese sauce, it's delightful!

Recipe contest entry: Phyllis Gaddis, Venice

6 tbsp. butter
8 cloves fresh garlic, minced
1 lb. fresh mushrooms, sliced thin with stems included
Dash salt (optional)
¼ lb. minced prosciutto, (¼ lb. crumbled cooked bacon may be substituted)
8 oz. white linguine
8 oz. green (spinach) linguine
1 cup light cream
¼ cup chicken broth
¼ cup grated Parmesan cheese, plus additional cheese for topping

Melt half the butter in large frying pan. Add garlic and saute until slightly browned. Add sliced mushrooms, sprinkle with a dash of salt and saute for 3 minutes, tossing occasionally, or until mushrooms are lightly browned. Remove from heat. In another pan saute proscuitto in remaining butter until browned. Remove from heat. Using two pots, prepare noodles according to package directions. The green pasta will take about 1 minute longer to cook than the white. If you drain the white noodles first, the green should be done and ready for draining when you are finished with the white. Combine both noodles in one bowl. Reheat skillet with garlic and mushrooms; add cream and chicken broth. When sauce simmers, add Parmesan cheese and stir to mix. Add both straw and hay noodles and toss to mix. Add prosciutto and toss again. Heat carefully, because high heat will change texture of Parmesan cheese. Just before serving, sprinkle with additional cheese.

As the local crops are harvested you can follow your nose to Garlic City, U.S.A.
MARJORIE RICE
Copley News Service

FAMILY FAVORITE LINGUINE AND CLAM SAUCE

This recipe, which originated in west central Italy, has been in the Robinson family for over 100 years. For variation, add 3 cups drained, canned Italian tomatoes to the sauce and simmer for 30 minutes before adding clams.

Recipe contest entry: John M. Robinson, Granada Hills

8 cloves fresh garlic
½ tsp. salt
½ tsp. white pepper
3 egg yolks
1 cup plus 4 tbsp. olive oil
2 tbsp. butter
3 tbsp. finely chopped shallots
3 tbsp. flour
2 to 2½ cups clam juice
3 to 4 cups coarsely chopped clams
1 cup chopped parsley
½ cup chopped basil
1 lb. linguine
Grated Romano cheese

Crush garlic in a mortar until it becomes a paste. Add salt, white pepper and egg yolks. Beat with a whisk until lemon colored. Continue to beat, adding olive oil a few drops at a time until 2 tbsp. have been added. Continue to beat, adding 1 cup olive oil in a thin stream until finished. Set sauce aside. In frying pan, heat remaining 2 tbsp. olive oil and butter; add shallots and saute over low heat until shallots are light golden. Add flour and continue cooking for 5 minutes, stirring constantly. Slowly add clam juice, stirring constantly, until well-blended; then cook 5 to 8 minutes more, stirring occasionally. Slowly add clam sauce to garlic sauce, stirring with a whisk to keep well-blended. Heat over low flame, stirring occasionally, until hot.

Add clams and continue to heat until hot again. Add parsley and basil. Heat until steaming and serve with freshly cooked linguine, prepared according to package instructions. Top with grated Romano cheese.

LINGUINE WITH WHITE CLAM SAUCE

Make a meal in minutes with this linguine topped with white clam sauce. Add a tossed green salad to round out this quickie dinner.

Recipe contest entry: Paul Dana, Sunnyvale

¾ cup olive oil
4 to 6 cloves fresh garlic
3 cans (6 to 7 oz. each) chopped clams
¼ tsp. salt and pepper
¼ tsp. thyme
1 lb. linguine
¼ cup chopped parsley

Heat oil in pan. Press garlic and cook until golden. Add clam juice from cans, salt, pepper and thyme. Let simmer very slowly. Add clams. Cook linguine. Add parsley to sauce five minutes before linguine is cooked.

FETTUCCINE FRAGALE

Garlic-buttered fettuccine, served with a creamy ricotta sauce, makes a superb pasta course or a hearty main dish. Louise Fragale sent her favorite recipe all the way from West Virginia for this cookbook.

Courtesy of: Louise Fragale, Clarksburg, West Virginia

¾ cup soft butter or margarine
2 tbsp. parsley flakes
1 tsp. crushed basil
1 carton (about 8 oz.) ricotta
¼ tsp. salt
½ tsp. pepper
⅔ cup warm milk
1 lb. fettuccine, thin noodles or spaghetti
3 cloves fresh garlic, minced
1 cup shredded or grated Romano or Parmesan cheese

Combine ¼ cup butter, parsley flakes and basil; blend in ricotta, salt and pepper. Stir in milk and blend well; keep warm. Cook noodles in large amount of boiling salted water until just tender; drain. Cook garlic in ½ cup butter for 1 to 2 minutes. Pour over noodles; toss lightly and quickly to coat well. Sprinkle with ½ cup cheese; toss again. Pile noodles on warm serving platter, and spoon the warm ricotta sauce over; sprinkle with the remaining cheese. Garnish with additional parsley, if desired. Makes 6 to 8 servings.

"So I decided, let's acknowledge our garlic industry," said Melone.
"Let's talk about the fact that garlic is great . . ."

ELIZABETH MEHREN, Washington *Post*

PASTA CON PESTO ALLA MELONE

Take a man of Italian descent who loves to cook, make him president of a community college which just happens to be in the center of a 90-mile radius of 90 percent of the nation's production of garlic and stand back! The Gilroy Garlic Festival could not have "happened" without the inspiration and creative mind of Dr. Rudy Melone and his foresight to know it was possible.

In this recipe from Dr. Melone's private collection he suggests a light, fine pasta to go with his gloriously garlicky pesto creation.

Courtesy of: Dr. Rudy Melone, President, Gavilan College;
Chairman, Gilroy Garlic Festival

1 cup grated fresh
  Parmesan cheese
2 cups fresh basil leaves
½ cup melted butter
10 to 20 cloves fresh garlic
  (depending on their size
  and your taste)
1 tbsp. pine nuts
¾ cup olive oil
Pasta (preferably capellini
  or vermicelli)

Using blender or food processor, grate enough Parmesan cheese to make one cup; add basil. Then add melted butter, followed by garlic, pine nuts and finally the oil. Allow each added ingredient to blend smoothly with the preceding ones, and let stand at least 1 hour. This is the pesto sauce. Prepare pasta according to package directions. Mix pesto with pasta fresh from the boiling water. Do not add too much pesto, but allow each person a chance to adjust flavor to taste, by adding more pesto if desired. Leftover pesto will last for quite a long while if refrigerated in a plastic container, but do not freeze.

A light salad with oil and vinegar dressing and a veal dish go great with this. Pasta con pesto is also a versatile accompaniment to a variety of dishes—meat, fish, poultry, etc.

SUPER MEAT SAUCE FOR PASTA

Sliced meat rolls add a new dimension to traditional pasta sauce. Use leftover sauce to make a delicious pizza.

Recipe contest entry: Becley Hill, Malibu

1 whole round steak, sliced ¼ inch thick
12 cloves fresh garlic, peeled and minced
2 cups chopped parsley
4 tbsp. oil
3 cans (8 oz. ea.) tomato sauce
2 tsp. sweet basil
1 tsp. oregano
1 tsp. salt
½ tsp. crushed red pepper
8 oz. spaghetti or other pasta
½ cup grated Parmesan cheese, or a mixture of Parmesan and Romano

Remove bone from steak and save. Cut steak into 4 pieces. Brush pieces with oil, top with garlic and parsley, dividing evenly. Roll up each piece of meat and secure by wrapping with sewing thread. Heat 4 tbsp. oil in heavy Dutch oven. Brown rolls of meat thoroughly. For added flavor, add the bone to the pan while meat is browning. Add the rest of the ingredients except pasta and cheese and cook over medium-low heat, stirring often, until tomato sauce has a slightly brown color. Cover and simmer 2 hours or until meat is very tender. Cook spaghetti according to package directions and drain. In a large, warmed serving bowl toss spaghetti with 1 cup sauce and ¼ cup cheese. Keep warm. Remove thread from meat rolls and slice. Top the spaghetti with meat and more sauce. Pass extra cheese. Makes 6 to 8 servings.

NOODLES ROMANOFF

Transform ordinary noodles into party fare in an instant using seasonings from your spice shelf.

2½ cups noodles
1 cup cottage cheese
1 cup dairy sour cream
1½ tsp. seasoned salt
1 tsp. instant minced onion
1 tsp. Worcestershire sauce
½ tsp. instant minced garlic
Dash cayenne or red pepper
⅓ cup grated Cheddar cheese

Cook noodles as directed on package and drain. Combine noodles with remaining ingredients except grated cheese. Put in buttered 1½-quart casserole; sprinkle top with grated cheese. Bake in 350°F oven 30 minutes or until cheese has melted. Makes 6 servings.

PASTA CON PESTO ALLA PELLICCIONE

Paul Pelliccione, one of the head chefs of Gourmet Alley, shares his fabulous recipe for pasta con pesto as it was prepared for the Garlic Festival.   *Courtesy of: Paul Pelliccione, Gilroy*

2 cups packed fresh basil leaves, washed and well drained

1½ cups grated Romano cheese, plus additional cheese, if desired

½ cup olive oil

½ cup melted butter

6 large cloves fresh garlic, crushed

1 lb. spaghetti, flat noodles or similar pasta, cooked according to package directions

Place basil, 1 cup of the cheese, oil, butter and garlic in blender. Begin blending, turning motor on and off. Push pesto down from sides of blender with rubber spatula and continue until you have a very coarse puree. Makes about 1½ cups pesto. Spoon 1 cup pesto sauce over freshly cooked spaghetti. Mix quickly with two forks. Add ½ cup cheese and mix. Serve with additional pesto sauce and cheese. Cover and refrigerate any leftover pesto up to a week, or freeze in small portions. The surface will darken when exposed to air, so stir the pesto before serving.

MARY ANN'S FETTUCCINE ZUCCHINI

Zucchini, tomatoes, garlic, herbs and spices make a savory sauce for fettuccine.   *Recipe contest entry: Mary Ann Rohm, Simi Valley*

3 tbsp. margarine

3 tbsp. olive oil

1 medium-sized sweet red onion, chopped

4 cloves fresh garlic, sliced

1 lb. sliced zucchini

1 tbsp. parsley

¼ tsp. oregano

¼ tsp. sweet basil

¼ tsp. thyme

⅛ tsp. marjoram

⅛ tsp. coarsely ground black pepper

⅛ tsp. ground red pepper

1 tsp. lemon juice

2 fresh tomatoes, chopped

1 lb. fettuccine

¼ cup Parmesan cheese

Melt margarine with olive oil in heavy saucepan over medium heat. Add onion and garlic and saute for 5 minutes. Add zucchini and saute 10 minutes. Add herbs and spices and saute until zucchini is almost tender. Then add lemon juice and tomatoes. Simmer. Cook fettuccine in salted boiling water until *al dente* and drain. Toss with zucchini mixture and top with Parmesan cheese. Serve at once.

WALNUT SAUCE FROM GARLIC COUNTRY

A rich mixture of nuts, olive oil, garlic and cheese makes a uniquely different topping for pasta.   *Recipe contest entry: Mrs. Bernarr Wilson, Gilroy*

12 oz. egg tagliarini
2 cups walnut meats
3 cloves fresh garlic
¼ cup butter
¼ cup olive oil
½ cup grated Parmesan
cheese plus
additional cheese, if
desired

Cook tagliarini as directed for about 9 minutes or until *al dente*. While tagliarini is cooking, mix walnut meats in blender with enough hot tagliarini water to make a paste. Add garlic, butter, olive oil and Parmesan cheese; blend, adding enough hot water to form desired consistency. Pour sauce over drained tagliarini; toss until well-coated and serve hot. Sprinkle on additional Parmesan cheese, if desired. Makes 4 to 6 servings.

SPAGHETTI JOSEPHINE

This recipe is a tribute to a lovely little Italian aunt-by-marriage who taught a North Carolina girl not to fear garlic. Aunt Jo hasn't been so well lately, and doesn't cook as often as she used to, but her style of cuisine lives on in a niece-in-law who turned to her husband one night and said, "How can I cook dinner—we're out of garlic!"

Recipe contest entry: Kathleen Kenney, Sausalito

1 medium head cauliflower,
separated into florets
1 lb. spaghetti
5 cloves fresh garlic, finely
minced
2 tbsp. olive oil
¼ cup minced parsley
½ cup butter
½ cup freshly grated
Parmesan cheese plus
additional cheese
Freshly ground pepper

Cook cauliflower in a large amount of boiling, salted water. When almost tender (about 10 to 12 minutes), add spaghetti and cook until spaghetti is *al dente*. While cauliflower is cooking, saute garlic in olive oil for about 1 minute. Add parsley and butter and cook over low heat until hot and bubbly. Drain spaghetti and cauliflower; add garlic butter and toss gently. Add grated cheese and toss again. Serve with additional grated cheese and freshly ground pepper.

GAGOOTZA

For your next party, try a different kind of pasta—spicy-hot with green chili salsa, California style.

Recipe contest entry: Carl Stockdale, Pasadena

Olive oil
3 large sweet white onions
2 to 3 bulbs fresh garlic, pressed
3 bunches minced parsley (just tops)
14 medium-sized zucchini, unpeeled, sliced ¼-inch thick
3 cans (7 oz. each) green chili salsa
3 lbs. Italian sausage, hot or mild
2 lbs. spaghetti
Garlic salt
About 2½ lbs. Mozzarella cheese, grated
1 can (about 7 oz.) ripe pitted olives, halved
1 can (about 8 oz.) button mushrooms

Cover bottom of electric skillet with ⅛ to ¼ inch olive oil. Slice onions ⅛ inch thick, separate into rings and saute in oil. Add garlic, parsley, zucchini and salsa; stir lightly and let simmer until zucchini becomes tender. Brown sausage in separate skillet and drain. Cook spaghetti 8 minutes in salted water and rinse with cool water. Grease six 8x10x2 pans with olive oil. Cover bottom of pans with ¾-inch layer of spaghetti; sprinkle lightly with garlic salt and add layer of sausage. Cover generously with zucchini mixture. Sprinkle grated cheese over top to thickness desired. Garnish with olives and mushrooms. Bake for 30 minutes at 350°F and serve immediately, or freeze without baking for future use; it keeps indefinitely. When ready to use, remove from freezer and bake for 45 minutes at 350°F. Serve with garlic toast, tossed green salad and beer or wine. Serves a bunch!

Meats

As early as 600 B.C., the Chinese were seasoning their sacrificial lambs with garlic to make them more acceptable to the gods. The tradition of garlic with lamb carries forth to this day. But garlic enhances not only lamb; it combines well with beef, pork, veal and nearly all other meats. Its flavor and aroma are a tribute not only to the gods, but to your dinner guests as well.

STEAK AND MUSHROOMS SAN JUAN

A lesser-priced cut of meat can be tender and delicious if prepared properly. This recipe for round steak capitalizes on the tenderizing effect of the wine and calls for a variety of seasonings to create a superb dish to serve over rice or noodles.

Courtesy of: Betty Angelino, Gilroy

2 lbs. top round steak
½ cup flour
Salt and pepper to taste
3 tbsp. olive oil
3 cloves fresh garlic, minced
2 tsp. oregano
1 tsp. rosemary
1 tsp. garlic salt
½ tsp. onion powder
½ tsp. thyme
1 cup water
½ cup red wine
1 cup sliced fresh mushrooms

Preheat electric fry pan to 420°F. Cut round steak into 2-inch strips. Roll in flour, salt and pepper. Add olive oil to fry pan; brown meat on both sides. Reduce heat to 220°F; add herbs and ½ cup water and steam for 20 minutes. Add remaining water, wine and mushrooms and cook 20 minutes more, or until tender. Check periodically, adding more water if needed. Remove meat from pan and add 1 to 2 tbsp. flour if necessary to thicken gravy. Serve with rice.

73

FLAUTAS AL BAU

Californians have so long enjoyed Mexican food like tacos, enchiladas, tamales and tostadas, it is sometimes difficult to realize that much of the rest of the U.S. population is just discovering these fine dishes. This recipe, for example, is quite easy to prepare and could serve as an appetizer or first course as well as an entree.

Recipe contest entry: Baudelia Leaderman, San Diego

Butter as needed
1½ lbs. ground beef
½ lb. chorizo (Mexican sausage, beef or pork)
2 large yellow onions, minced
3 large semi-hot Jalapeno chiles, finely diced
4 medium tomatoes, cut into 1-inch cubes
1 tbsp. paprika
Salt and pepper to taste
Juice of 1 lemon
2 tbsp. dairy sour cream
16 corn tortillas

Melt enough butter in a large skillet to cook the beef, chorizo, onions and chiles (chorizo should be mashed into mixture); cook until beef has browned and chorizo separates. Add tomatoes, paprika, salt, pepper and garlic; mix together. Turn flame to low and let simmer about 10 minutes. Remove from heat and drain off half of liquid. Mix in lemon juice; fold in sour cream. Let mixture stand 5 minutes to blend flavors. Divide mixture evenly into tortillas and roll tightly, using toothpick to hold each together. Fry tortillas in butter until semi-brown. Remove and serve hot.

TIJUANA JAIL CHILI

Like all border towns, Tijuana, Mexico, just across the line from San Diego, has a colorful, if somewhat shady, reputation. It's hard to believe such delightful fare would be served in any of the prisons there, but regardless of how this dish got its name, it's worth preparing. Serve it with a tossed salad and plenty of cold beer.

Courtesy of Louis Bonesio, Jr., Gilroy

⅛ lb. suet, finely chopped
3 lbs. round steak, coarsely cubed
3 cloves fresh garlic, minced
6 tbsp. chili powder
1 tbsp. ground oregano
1 tbsp. crushed cumin seed
1 tbsp. salt
½ to 1 tbsp. cayenne
1 tsp. Tabasco sauce
1½ quarts water
½ cup white cornmeal

In Dutch oven fry suet until crisp; add steak cubes and brown. Add seasonings and water; heat to boil. Then cover and simmer 1½ hours. Skim off fat; stir in cornmeal and continue to simmer, uncovered, for 30 minutes. Stir occasionally. Serve in bowls with either beans and tortillas or cornbread.

GILROY CHILI

When this recipe for chili was served at a Gilroy barbecue to accompany grilled steaks, everyone declared it outstanding and many had second and third helpings.

Recipe contest entry: David B. Swope, Redondo Beach

3 cloves fresh garlic, minced
2 large onions, finely chopped
2 tbsp. olive oil
2 lbs. ground beef
1 can (4 oz.) green chiles
1 cup canned stewed tomatoes
2 cups beef stock
1 tbsp. chili powder
1 tbsp. ground cumin
1½ tsp. MSG (optional)
1 tsp. salt
¼ tsp. pepper

In large skillet slowly brown garlic and onions in olive oil; stir and cook until tender. Heat skillet to hot, add meat and cook until done. Add all other ingredients. Cover and reduce heat. Cook about 45 minutes more. Either remove grease or add a small amount cornstarch to absorb it.

TAMALE PARTY PIE

Tamale pie has wide popular appeal. This recipe goes together easily and will serve about 20 people. If you prepare it for your family and have some left over, freeze it for use another time or in small individual portions for family members to prepare for themselves on the cook's night out!

Courtesy of: Florence Sillano, Gilroy

1 can (1 lb.) creamed corn
2 cans (8 oz. each) hot sauce
2 large onions, finely chopped
1 cup salad oil
2 tbsp. chili powder
4 cloves fresh garlic, minced
2 cups polenta (cornmeal)
1 pint milk
3 eggs, beaten
1 can pitted ripe olives, including juice
Salt and pepper to taste
1½ lbs. lean ground beef

Mix all ingredients and place in a 16x11x2½ baking dish. Bake ½ hour at 350°F. Reduce heat to 300°F and continue to bake 45 minutes longer.

GREEN GARLIC CHILI

Much like a Chile Verde, this recipe for Green Garlic Chili is easy to prepare and quite good.   *Recipe contest entry: Wesley L. Minor, Seal Beach.*

2 lbs. beef (use any desired cut)
½ cup olive oil
3 bulbs fresh garlic
6 fresh green chiles
½ tsp. salt
½ tsp. white pepper
1 large onion
3 large green tomatoes

Cut beef into slices or ½-inch cubes. Heat oil in skillet and cook beef until well-done and tender. Separate bulbs into cloves and peel. Place whole cloves in skillet and cook until tender. Add green chiles and onions. Dice green tomatoes and add to skillet. Add the remainder of the seasonings and cook, covered, to retain as much juice as possible.

TRIPE A LA LOUIS

If you haven't tried tripe, here's a recipe to give you inspiration. Simmered with tomatoes, white wine, beef stock, vegetables, garlic and spices, this dish will make your kitchen smell heavenly as it cooks. A little chopped cilantro and oregano are pleasing garnishes.

Courtesy of: Louis Bonesio, Jr, Gilroy

3 lbs. honeycomb tripe
3 tbsp. olive oil
1 large onion, sliced
2 large carrots, sliced
1 large bell pepper, cut into ¾-inch pieces
½ cup tomato puree
1 cup chopped stewed tomatoes
2 cups dry white wine
1 cup beef stock or bouillon
1 bay leaf
4 cloves fresh garlic, crushed
4 to 6 dashes Tabasco sauce
½ tsp. fine black pepper
¼ tsp. thyme
1 can (1 lb.) hominy
Cilantro, chopped
Oregano

Cut tripe into 1-by-2-inch pieces and boil in lightly salted water for 15 minutes. Set aside to drain. Saute in a heavy Dutch oven with olive oil, onion, carrots and bell pepper for 5 to 15 minutes. Add tomato puree, stewed tomatoes, white wine, beef stock or bouillon, bay leaf, garlic, Tabasco, pepper, thyme and hominy. Add the tripe to the Dutch oven and simmer 2½ to 3 hours. Serve with chopped cilantro and a little oregano to garnish. Serves 6 hungry eaters!!

BEEF TERIYAKI

No garlic cookbook would be complete without a beef teriyaki recipe because garlic is so important to the flavor of this oriental marinade. Alternate the meat with pineapple chunks for an eye-appealing presentation.

1 lb. sirloin beef, cut 1 inch thick
¾ cup soy sauce
¼ cup dark brown sugar, packed
2 tbsp. lemon juice
1 tsp. ground ginger
½ tsp. garlic powder
½ tsp. onion salt

Cut meat into bite-sized cubes. Combine remaining ingredients; pour over beef cubes and let stand at room temperature one hour or in refrigerator several hours. Thread cubes of meat onto a skewer. (Pineapple chunks may be alternated with the beef cubes.) Broil about 3 inches from heat 10 to 12 minutes, turning once, or cook over grill or hibachi. Serve hot as an appetizer or with rice as a main course.

SHERRIED OXTAILS

On a cold, rainy night, these Sherried Oxtails will offer warming comfort. The meat is simmered with vegetables to tender perfection in a thick, bubbling broth.   *Courtesy of: Louis Bonesio, Jr. Gilroy*

¼ cup flour
3 tsp. paprika
1 tsp. salt
4 lbs. oxtails, cut into serving-size pieces
¼ cup butter or margarine
2 cups boiling water
½ lb. sliced mushrooms
1 red pepper, thinly sliced and seeded
2 large onions, thinly sliced
3 cloves fresh garlic, crushed
2 beef bouillon cubes
2 vegetable bouillon cubes
2 tsp. curry powder
1 cup dry sherry or tomato juice

Blend flour, paprika and salt. Coat oxtails with this mixture and reserve remaining flour. In large frying pan with lid, melt butter. Brown floured oxtails in melted butter on all sides. Add boiling water; cover and simmer for about an hour. Stir in mushrooms, red pepper, onions, garlic, beef and vegetable bouillon cubes and curry powder. Cover again and continue cooking for about two hours longer, or until meat is very tender. Blend in sherry or tomato juice and simmer uncovered for about 15 minutes longer. In small bowl, gradually stir a little of the cooking liquid into reserved seasoned flour to form a smooth paste; blend flour paste into oxtails and cook, stirring constantly, until thickened and bubbling. Makes 4 to 6 servings.

LIMAS AND SAUSAGE ITALIANO

Spicy sausage and herbs blend well with lima beans to make a low-cost and very appealing casserole.

1 lb. bulk Italian (or other spicy) sausage
¼ cup chopped onion
½ tsp. garlic powder
¼ tsp. rosemary leaves
¼ tsp. thyme leaves
1 can (8 oz.) tomato sauce
2 cans (1 lb. each) lima beans
¼ cup butter
1 cup dry bread crumbs
1 tbsp. parsley flakes

Crumble sausage; add onion and garlic powder. Saute in a skillet until sausage is browned, stirring and breaking up with a fork while cooking. Crush rosemary leaves and add to sausage, along with thyme leaves and tomato sauce. Simmer 15 minutes. Drain limas; add to sausage mixture. Stir to mix well. Transfer to a 1½-quart casserole. Melt butter; stir into bread crumbs and parsley flakes, tossing lightly. Spoon over top of bean mixture. Bake in 350°F oven 1 hour or until crumbs are golden. Makes 4 to 6 servings.

GARLIC FRITTATA

For brunch or a light supper, this frittata is a snap to fix and the flavor is superb. Try serving it with steamed artichokes or a green salad and a chilled California white wine, like Chablis.

Recipe contest entry: Anne T. Kahn, Newark

8 eggs
½ cup milk
½ cup grated Parmesan cheese
2 tbsp. butter
4 cloves fresh garlic, minced
½ cup chopped onion
1 to 4 oz. Polish sausage or garlic sausage, chopped
4 large potatoes, shredded
4 oz. Cheddar cheese, shredded

Beat together eggs, milk and Parmesan cheese; set aside. In large skillet, over medium-high heat, melt butter and saute garlic, onion, sausage and potatoes for about 5 minutes or until tender. Reduce heat to medium. Pour egg mixture into pan and cook, without stirring, until eggs are almost set. Sprinkle Cheddar cheese over top of frittata. Let cook on top of stove for about 1 more minute. Place pan under broiler and broil about 6 inches from heat until top is bubbly and slightly browned. Cut in wedges to serve.

CONEJO A LA CHILINDRON   *Sauteed Rabbit*

Tender rabbit, cooked the Spanish way, is an old country recipe submitted by a San Mateo family. You may want to include it in your family's cooking traditions after you taste its remarkably rich flavor.

Recipe contest entry: Fernandez-Carozzi family, San Mateo

2 to 3 lb. rabbit, cut into 6 to 8 serving pieces
Salt to taste
Freshly ground black pepper
¼ cup olive oil
2 large onions, cut lengthwise in half and then into ¼-inch wide strips
1 tsp. fresh garlic, finely chopped
3 sweet red or green peppers, seeded and cut lengthwise into ¼-inch wide strips
½ cup smoked ham, finely chopped
6 tomatoes, peeled, seeded and finely chopped
6 pitted black olives, halved
6 pitted green olives, halved

Rinse and pat rabbit pieces dry with paper towels; sprinkle liberally with salt and a little pepper. In heavy 10- to 12-inch skillet, heat oil over moderate heat until light haze forms; saute rabbit and as pieces become a rich brown transfer them to a plate. Add onions, garlic, pepper strips and ham to oil remaining in skillet. Stirring frequently, cook for 8 to 10 minutes over moderate heat until vegetables are soft, but not brown. Add tomatoes; raise heat and cook briskly until most of the liquid in the pan evaporates and mixture is thick enough to hold its shape lightly in a spoon. Return rabbit to skillet, turning pieces with a spoon to coat them evenly with sauce. Cover tightly and simmer over low heat for 25 to 30 minutes or until rabbit is tender. Stir in olives, and adjust seasonings to taste.

GARLIC IS GOLD
FOR GILROY
Sacramento *Bee*

GARLIC BEEF ENCHILADAS

Although at first glance this recipe may seem complicated, it is actually easy to prepare. The sauce and meat filling can even be made ahead and refrigerated. Reheat slightly when ready to use.

Courtesy of: Julie Gutierrez, Gilroy

Sauce
4 cloves fresh garlic, minced
3 tbsp. shortening
1 can (28 oz.) red chili sauce
3 tbsp. flour
1 can (8 oz.) tomato sauce

Filling
1 lb. ground chuck
2 cloves fresh garlic, minced
Salt and pepper to taste

Enchiladas
1 cup shortening
2 cloves fresh garlic, minced
1 medium-sized onion, finely chopped
4 cups grated Cheddar cheese
2 cans (6 oz. each) medium pitted ripe olives
2 dozen fresh corn tortillas

To prepare sauce: Saute garlic until golden in hot shortening in large saucepan. Add can of chili sauce and lower heat. Put flour in separate bowl and stir in can of tomato sauce until smooth. Pour into chili sauce mixture and stir over medium heat until slightly thickened. Set aside; let cool.

To prepare meat filling: In medium skillet over low heat, saute chuck with garlic, salt and pepper until chuck is browned. Set aside.

To prepare enchiladas: Heat shortening in large skillet over medium-high heat. Carefully dip 1 tortilla at a time into hot shortening, frying each side for 5 seconds. Dip fried tortilla into cooled enchilada sauce and place on flat plate. After you have prepared 6 tortillas, fill center of each with meat, garlic, onion, cheese, and olives (reserving some cheese and olives to sprinkle on top). Roll up tortillas.

Pour half the sauce in a large baking dish. Then arrange filled tortillas seam side down in sauce. Repeat, 6 tortillas at a time, until all have been cooked and assembled. Pour remaining sauce over tortillas. Sprinkle with cheese and garnish with olives. Bake 15 to 20 minutes at 350°F until cheese is melted. Makes 2 dozen.

GARLIC FESTIVAL BELL PEPPER AND STEAK SANDWICHES

The aroma of gently sauteeing garlic brought on hunger pangs and set mouths watering. Those who attended the Garlic Festival are still talking about the Pepper Beefsteak Sandwiches served in Gourmet Alley. Chef Lou Trinchero and his team of cooks served 700 pounds of top sirloin, 250 pounds of green peppers and 750 loaves of French bread. Thank goodness Lou has worked the recipe down to one which will "feed 4 generously." You'll want to have plenty because they are unbelievably delicious.   *Courtesy of: Lou Trinchero, Gilroy*

8 bell peppers, seeded and sliced in quarters
1 medium-sized onion, chopped
3 cloves fresh garlic, minced
Salt and pepper to taste
Olive oil
¾ lb. top sirloin steak, barbecued or broiled to desired degree of doneness
8 French rolls, halved and basted with garlic butter
Garlic butter (see Miscellaneous section)

In skillet saute peppers, onion, garlic and salt and pepper in olive oil until tender. Brush rolls with garlic butter and heat in the oven or toast lightly under the broiler or over the barbecue. Slice steak thin and place on bottom half of roll. Top with pepper-garlic mixture and other half of roll. Makes 8 sandwiches.

CRUSTY LAMB CON AJO

Tere Gonzales de Usabiaga from Celaya, Mexico, whose husband is a garlic grower, shares this exquisite method of preparing lamb that brings out a robust, garlicky flavor.
Courtesy of: Tere Gonzales de Usabiaga, Celaya, Mexico

3 extra-large bulbs of fresh garlic (approx. 6 oz.)
¼ cup minced fresh parsley
¼ cup oil
Leg of lamb

Separate garlic into cloves and remove skins. Place garlic, parsley and oil in a blender or food processor and mix until a paste is formed. Remove excess fat from meat. Spread garlic mixture on all sides of meat. Bake uncovered in 350°F oven 30 minutes per pound. This garlic mixture can also be used on other cuts of meat, such as rack of lamb, pork loin roasts, prime rib of beef, etc.

TORTILLA LOAF

Gilroy's Spanish/Mexican heritage can be seen, not only in the names of streets, ranches and public buildings, but in the types of food prepared by its citizens. Dishes like this tortilla loaf, for example, utilize ingredients native to Mexico and combine them into a wonderful supper dish.   *Courtesy of: Rose Emma Pelliccione, Gilroy*

1 large onion, chopped
3 cloves fresh garlic, minced
¼ cup oil
1½ to 2 lbs. ground beef
2 cans (8 oz. each) hot sauce
1 can (10½ oz.) beef consomme
1 can (7½ oz.) pitted ripe olives, sliced
2 tbsp. wine vinegar
2 tbsp. chili powder
1½ cups grated sharp Cheddar cheese
1 dozen corn tortillas

Saute onion and garlic in oil; add ground beef and saute until redness disappears and meat is crumbled. Add other ingredients, except cheese and tortillas. Cook for a few minutes to blend flavors. If sauce is too thick, thin with a little water. Place tortillas, sauce and cheese in layers, ending with sauce and cheese on top. Bake for 45 mintues at 350°F.

PACIFIC POT ROAST

There is no question but that garlic improves the flavor of a simple pot roast, and tomato juice enriches the gravy which tastes very good served over rice.

Recipe contest entry: Elaine R. Muse, San Diego

1 boneless rolled chuck roast
8 cloves fresh garlic
1½ tsp. salt
½ tsp. black pepper
¼ tsp. red pepper
Oil for browning
1½ cups water
1 large onion, chopped
Flour
Water
1 tbsp. Worcestershire sauce
¼ cup tomato juice
Salt to taste

Make 8 slits in roast at random intervals. Into each slit insert one whole clove garlic and rub roast with a mixture of salt and pepper. Lightly coat bottom of a Dutch oven with oil. Brown meat well on all sides.

Add water and onion; cover and simmer 2 hours or until tender. When roast is done, remove to platter and thicken gravy with flour mixed with water. Season gravy with three remaining ingredients. Slice roast and serve with gravy over cooked rice.

BEEF STEW BONESIO

Nearly everyone has a favorite beef stew recipe. This one produces a gravy rich with the combined flavors of wine and herbs, which is equally good with both the meat and the vegetables.

Courtesy of: Louis Bonesio, Jr., Gilroy

1½ lbs. lean beef stew meat, cut into 1½-inch cubes
3 tbsp. flour
3 tbsp. polyunsaturated oil
½ cup dry red wine
1½ cups boiling water
2½ medium onions, sliced
3 medium carrots, cut into ½-inch slices
3 cups potatoes, peeled and cut into 1-inch cubes
½ stalk celery, sliced into ½-inch slices
3 medium cloves fresh garlic
1/8 tsp. marjoram
1/8 tsp. dry crushed oregano
1/8 tsp. ground sage
1 tsp. thyme
2 tbsp. chopped parsley
1 tsp. freshly ground pepper
½ lb. whole small mushrooms

Remove visible fat from meat. Dredge well in flour; brown lightly in oil in a 4-qt. Dutch oven. Gradually add wine and enough boiling water just to cover meat. Reduce heat and simmer, covered, for 1 hour. Add onions, carrots, potatoes, celery and garlic, marjoram, oregano, sage, thyme and parsley. Continue to simmer 30 minutes. Remove from heat and let stand 15 minutes. Skim fat off top. Add pepper and mushrooms and bring to boil; reduce heat and simmer 10 more minutes. Garnish with additional chopped parsley. Makes 4 to 6 servings.

CHARCOAL GRILLED STEAK

For best flavor, most barbecue chefs recommend marinating steaks for several hours before cooking.

4 club steaks, cut 1 inch thick
½ cup salad oil
2 tbsp. lemon juice
1 tsp. onion salt
1 tsp. Worcestershire sauce
¾ tsp. garlic powder
½ tsp. seasoned salt
¼ tsp. black pepper

Place steaks in shallow baking dish. Combine remaining ingredients and pour over steaks, coating all sides. Marinate several hours in refrigerator, turning once. Place on grill and sear on both sides. Raise grill to about 5 inches from coals. Cook 15 minutes, turning once, or until desired degree of doneness is reached.

VEAL SHANKS WITH GARLIC

Ann Epstein, third place winner in the Garlic Recipe Contest and Cook-off cooked with *four whole bulbs* of garlic in her recipe for veal shanks. Garlic and veal cook together in a wine sauce for about an hour or so and when ready, the garlic is gathered in a dish and offered to guests to spread, like butter, on toasty bread to eat with the meat. Be sure to select a robust red wine to go with it.

Recipe contest winner: Ann Epstein, North Hollywood

3 hind leg veal shanks, each cut into 3 or 4 one-inch pieces
½ cup oil (corn, peanut, soy, sesame, olive or a mixture)
3 large onions, thickly sliced
1 or 2 large carrots, thickly sliced
Bouquet garni
1 cup dry white wine
2 to 3 cups brown veal stock or beef or chicken broth, enough to cover the meat
Salt and pepper to taste
4 bulbs of fresh garlic
Fresh chopped parsley
Bread, cut in thick slices and toasted

Nervously, Epstein eyed her competitors, "Omigod," she said. "These are heavy-duty garlic freaks."
Oakland *Tribune*

In a large braising pot, brown veal shanks in hot oil until golden on all sides. Remove meat. Into hot oil, add onions, carrots, bouquet garni and toss until soft and golden brown. Spoon off as much fat as possible. In the same pot, arrange cooked vegetables, then veal shanks, then wine. Reduce wine completely, taking care not to burn meat and vegetables. Add the veal stock or meat broth. Bring to a boil. Have ready all the cloves from the 4 bulbs of garlic separated, peeled and mashed with a knife or mallet. Add these to simmering meat. Add salt and pepper. Cover with a layer of foil the sides of which have been turned up so that the steam will not dilute the sauce. Cover with pot lid. Bake in 325°F oven for 1 to 1½ hours, until meat will be done when it pulls easily away from the bones. There should be between 1½ to 2 cups of rich, thick sauce left. If more, reduce till required amount is reached. Onions and carrots can be left in the sauce as is, removed, pureed and added back, or removed entirely. Place meat on a pretty platter. Sprinkle with parsley. Gather all mashed garlic cloves and place in a dish. Serve meat and toasted slices of bread spread with mashed garlic. Because of the lengthy cooking, the garlic loses much of its pungency and becomes very rich and buttery in texture.

LARRY'S FAVORITE BEEF IN BEER

"When Larry comes to town, he always shows up with a six-pack of beer, a juicy round steak and pleads with me to fix this dish," explains Phyllis Gaddis about her recipe contribution. "Whether or not it's my recipe or the rest of the six-pack that makes his eyes shine when I serve it, I'll never know, but he can count on my having the rest of the ingredients!"   *Recipe contest entry: Phyllis Gaddis, Venice*

1 round steak, fat trimmed
  away
½ cup chopped parsley
1 bay leaf, crumbled
½ tsp. thyme
¼ tsp. celery seed
  Pinch of sage
2 tbsp. vegetable oil
3 tbsp. prepared mustard
2 large onions, chopped
  Salt and pepper to taste
5 cloves fresh garlic,
  minced
12 oz. beer
1 cup dairy sour cream

Cut steak into 4 portions, or slice across the grain into ¼-inch slices. Mix parsley, bay leaf, thyme, celery seed and sage together and place in cheesecloth bag, tied with string. Cut tail of string short after knotting. In large skillet, heat oil and saute steak portions or slices on one side, spreading mustard on top side. Turn and saute mustard-topped side. Only sear the meat on high heat. Quickly add onions; stir-fry 1 minute and lower heat. Add salt and pepper to taste, then add garlic. Pour in beer slowly, and add spice bag. Return heat to simmer, cover and reduce heat to low. Cook for 1 hour for 4 steak portions, and about 30 minutes if steak is sliced, adding additional beer if needed. When the beer has reduced considerably, about 5 minutes before the end of the cooking time, stir in sour cream, mixing well. Raise heat slightly and serve when sauce is hot. Needless to say, we serve beer with Larry's Favorite Beef, and a large salad of greens, cut tomatoes, and Bermuda onions sliced very thin with a simple oil and vinegar dressing, and sesame seeds sprinkled on top.

LENA'S MEATBALLS

The combination of pork and beef helps to keep these meatballs moist and juicy no matter how you choose to cook them.

Recipe contest entry: Lena Lico, Hollister

1 lb. ground beef
½ lb. ground pork (lean)
⅓ cup grated Romano or Parmesan cheese
4 slices bread, soaked in water and squeezed tightly
2 eggs
5 cloves fresh garlic, minced
1 medium onion, finely chopped
1 tbsp. chopped parsley
2 tsp. salt
1 tsp. oregano
½ tsp. black pepper

Combine all ingredients and mix well. Shape into balls. These can be fried, cooked in the oven or dropped into hot spaghetti sauce.

DIANE'S BARBECUED MEXICAN LAMB CHOPS

Bathe loin lamb chops in a lemony marinade infused with aromatic herbs for a Mexican-style barbecue.

Recipe contest entry: Diane Truesdell, San Jose

⅓ cup Chablis
½ cup oil
¼ cup fresh lemon juice
3 large cloves fresh garlic, minced
2 tbsp. brown sugar
2 tsp. onions, minced
2 tsp. cilantro leaves
½ tsp. ground black pepper
½ tsp. salt
¼ tsp. basil
¼ tsp. rosemary
1/8 tsp. oregano
8 thickly cut lamb chops, center cut or shoulder

Combine all ingredients except lamb chops, and mix thoroughly. Pour over lamb chops and marinate overnight. Barbecue over hot coals until chops are well-browned and tender. Serve with green salad, hot steamed rice, zucchini cooked with basil and red Spanish onions, and crisp French bread.

GOOD 'N GARLICKY KEBABS

Use this zesty marinade for your next barbecue. Grilled lamb and vegetables make a mouth-watering meal-in-one.

¾ cup dry red wine
¼ cup olive oil
¼ cup red wine vinegar
1 onion, chopped
5 cloves fresh garlic,
   pressed
1 tsp. salt
1 tsp. rosemary
1 tsp. Worcestershire sauce
1 bay leaf
1/8 tsp. pepper
2 lbs. lamb, cut into
   1½-inch cubes
16 mushrooms
16 cherry tomatoes
1 large green pepper, cut
   into 12 chunks
1 large onion, cut into 12
   chunks

Combine wine, oil, vinegar, onion, garlic and seasonings. Marinate lamb overnight in this mixture. Divide lamb into four portions and thread on 4 skewers. Divide vegetables into four portions and thread on 4 skewers. Grill lamb four inches from coals about 20 to 25 minutes, turning to cook all sides. Add vegetables the last 10 to 12 minutes. Baste meat and vegetables with marinade during the cooking process. Makes 4 servings.

To simplify preparation of marinade, combine all marinade ingredients in a food processor. The garlic can be left whole and the onion can be cut in large chunks. Process with quick on-and-off bursts until onion has been pureed.

HERBED MINUTE STEAKS

Marinating in a wine and herb sauce before grilling does wonders for minute steaks, and the topping of sour cream and paprika dresses up what otherwise might be considered a plain cut of meat.

1 cup salad oil
½ cup red wine
¾ tsp. garlic powder
½ tsp. onion powder
½ tsp. celery salt
½ tsp. salt
½ tsp. oregano
½ tsp. basil
¼ tsp. black pepper
¼ tsp. MSG (optional)
   Dash nutmeg
6 minute or cube steaks
½ cup dairy sour cream
   Paprika

Combine all ingredients, except steaks, sour cream and paprika, in glass or enameled flat pan; mix well. Add steaks and marinate 1 hour, turning several times. Remove from marinade; pan-fry in hot skillet, or broil just until browned on each side. Top each steak with a spoon of sour cream and sprinkle with paprika. Makes 6 servings.

ROAST TENDERLOIN SAN BENITO

The technique of marinating this roast in lemon juice and oil a half hour or so before cooking helps to ensure that the meat will be juicy and tender when served.

1 4-lb. beef tenderloin
¼ cup lemon juice
¼ cup oil
1 tsp. MSG or ½ tsp. salt
1 tsp. coarse black pepper
1 tsp. herb seasoning
1 tsp. powdered
  horseradish
½ tsp. garlic powder
¼ tsp. mace

Marinate roast in mixture of lemon juice and oil 30 minutes to 1 hour, turning once or twice. Remove meat from marinade. Combine seasonings and rub over meat. Roast in 450°F oven approximately 45 minutes for rare, or until meat thermometer registers desired degree of doneness.

PAJARO PEPPERED TENDERLOIN

A gourmet steak, peppery, pungent, with a zesty sauce. Excellent served with wild rice and sauteed mushrooms.

6 slices beef tenderloin, cut
  1 inch thick
¾ tsp. garlic salt
½ tsp. salt
¼ tsp. MSG (optional)
  Coarse black pepper
3 tbsp. butter
1 tsp. flour
½ tsp. beef flavor base
¼ cup hot water
2 tbsp. Sauterne
¼ tsp. shredded green
  onions

Trim off most of the outside fat, and slash remaining fat every inch or so to prevent curling. Season steak with a mixture of garlic salt, salt and MSG. Sprinkle pepper generously over each side and press down with knife. Saute in butter about 4 minutes on each side. Remove meat to heated serving platter. To essence in skillet add flour and beef flavor base, stirring to mix well; then add hot water, Sauterne and shredded green onions. Bring to a boil and spoon sauce over steak. Serve immediately. Makes 6 servings.

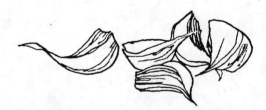

"I love garlic so I use quite a bit," says fireman Bob Dixon of Santa Cruz . . . "I have to vent myself," says Dixon, "I see people's faces light up after I feed them. That's my reward."

MARY PHILLIPS, San Jose *Mercury*

GILROY MEAT-AND-POTATOES QUICHE

Another finalist from the Garlic Recipe Contest and Cook-off, this fireman who gets lots of practice cooking at the firehouse, claims this dish is a favorite. When you taste it you'll know why.

Recipe contest finalist: Bob Dixon, Santa Cruz

Crust
- 1 lb. ground beef
- ¾ cup bread crumbs
- 1 egg
- 1 clove fresh garlic, minced
- 2 tbsp. Worcestershire sauce
- 2 tbsp. chopped fresh basil
- ½ tsp. pepper

Combine all ingredients and press into a 9-inch pie pan. Bake in 350°F oven for 15 minutes. Remove from oven and set aside.

Filling
- 3 cloves fresh garlic, minced
- ½ cup diced onion
- 2 tbsp. oil
- 3 medium potatoes, peeled, cooked and sliced
- 4 oz. Cheddar cheese, cubed
- 1 can (4 oz.) green chiles, chopped
- 1 tsp. salt
- ½ tsp. pepper

Saute garlic and onion in oil for 5 minutes. Combine potatoes, (reserving enough to make ½ cup mashed for topping) and cheese with garlic and onion, chiles, salt and pepper. Mix well and spread over the beef crust.

Topping
- ½ cup potatoes, mashed with ½ cup milk
- 2 oz. Cheddar cheese
- 3 cloves fresh garlic, minced
- 1 egg
- 1 tsp. dry mustard

Combine all the above ingredients and pour over the filling. Bake in 350°F oven for 25 to 30 minutes.

GARLIC MAY BE A LOT OF THINGS, BUT NOW IT'S CAUSE FOR CELEBRATION

Chicago *Tribune*

SPIT-ROASTED ROLLED RIB

This rolled rib roast is seasoned with a delicious combination of seasonings which can be varied by adding either 1 teaspoon crushed rosemary leaves or ½ teaspoon crushed thyme leaves.

1 4- to 5-lb. rolled rib roast
2 tsp. seasoned salt
1 tsp. salt
¾ tsp. garlic powder
½ tsp. onion salt
½ tsp. coarse black pepper
¼ tsp. ginger
¼ tsp. dry mustard

Trim off most of the outside fat from roast. Combine seasonings and rub into all surfaces of the roast. Place on spit, 5 to 6 inches from coals, and cook 1½ hours or until desired degree of doneness is reached. Makes 6 to 8 servings.

SCALOPPINE AL LIMONE

The term *scaloppine* describes the thin slices of veal which make this dish distinctive. Here lemon is used instead of wine and can be increased if a more *picante* flavor is desired.

1 lb. veal, cut for
  scaloppine
2 tbsp. flour
2 tbsp. salad oil
1 can (4 oz.) sliced
  mushrooms
¾ cup water
¼ cup onion, minced
2 tbsp. green pepper,
  chopped
1 tbsp. lemon juice
1½ tsp. seasoned salt
1 tsp. garlic powder
¼ tsp. black pepper
¼ tsp. nutmeg

Dredge veal with flour. Saute on both sides in hot oil until well-browned. Add remaining ingredients, including liquid from mushrooms. Cover and simmer 10 minutes. Serve from platter attractively garnished with tomato wedges, potato cakes, parsley or paprika-rimmed slices of lemon. Makes 2 to 4 servings.

THE SWEET,
GARLICKY SMELL OF
SUCCESS IN GILROY
San Francisco *Examiner*

VEAL PARMIGIANA

Parmigiana is the Italian word for Parmesan, the cheese which comes from Parma, Italy, and which has found such acceptance throughout the world because it grates and cooks better than almost any other cheese. Its flavor combines well with garlic and other seasonings in this well-known and popular dish.

Sauce
  1 can (6 oz.) tomato paste
  1 can (6 oz.) water
  1 tbsp. butter
  1 tbsp. brown sugar
  1 tsp. Worcestershire sauce
  1 tsp. seasoned salt
  ½ tsp. garlic powder
  ½ tsp. Italian seasoning
  ¼ tsp. oregano
  1/8 tsp. MSG (optional)

Mix all ingredients together. Cook until sauce has thickened, stirring constantly. Set aside.

  2 lbs. veal cutlets
  2 tsp. seasoned salt
  ¼ tsp. black pepper
  2 eggs
  1 cup fine dry bread crumbs
  ½ cup olive oil
  ¼ cup grated Parmesan cheese
  ½ lb. Mozzarella cheese

Have cutlets sliced ½ inch thick; cut into serving-size pieces or leave whole. Add seasoned salt and pepper to eggs; beat lightly. Dip cutlets into egg mixture, then into bread crumbs. Brown on both sides in hot oil. Place cutlets in 8x13x1¾-inch baking dish. Pour sauce over meat and sprinkle with Parmesan cheese. Cover, using aluminum foil if necessary, and bake in 350°F oven 30 minutes or until tender. Remove cover and top with slices of Mozzarella cheese. Continue baking until cheese melts. Makes 4 to 6 servings.

ANNABELLE'S PORTUGUESE PORK IN ORANGE JUICE

We are pleased to present two time-honored Portuguese recipes from the wife of Ralph Santos, local garlic grower and shipper. You can give pork an exquisitely different flavor when you cook it Portuguese style.   *Courtesy of: Annabelle Santos, Gilroy*

1 cup Burgundy
1 cup water
¼ cup orange juice
12 cloves fresh garlic, crushed
1 tsp. ground cumin
½ tsp. each cloves, allspice, cinnamon (scant)
1 tsp. salt
¼ tsp. ground pepper
Pork loin roast or other cut of pork of your choice

Mix together all ingredients except meat. Pour mixture over pork and marinate for 48 hours, then drain off liquid and reserve. The pork may be roasted or barbecued. Brush meat with marinade while cooking.

ANNABELLE'S PORK IN VINEGAR

3 cups water
1 cup wine vinegar
1 tbsp. salt
½ tsp. ground pepper
6 to 8 cloves fresh garlic, crushed
½ tsp. ground cumin
½ tsp. paprika

Combine all ingredients and follow the directions as above.

ADOBO

Filipino cooks have a way with garlic, as demonstrated in this classic pork adobo. It's easy to prepare and has a lovely, piquant sauce.
Recipe contest entry: Jean Ballton, Gilroy

3 cloves fresh garlic, minced
3 lbs. pork, cut in 2-inch cubes
15 whole black peppercorns
1 bay leaf
½ cup plus 1 tbsp. vinegar
6 tbsp. soy sauce
2 tbsp. sugar

Mix all ingredients together in large pot and simmer 1 hour. Serve with rice and green vegetables. Makes 4 servings.

RAGOUT OF LAMB

Simmer lamb with herbs and vegetable chunks for a classic stew.

2 lbs. lean lamb, cubed
1 tbsp. oil
1 cup chopped onion
1 tsp. seasoned salt
1 tsp. celery salt
1 tsp. beef flavor base
¾ tsp. instant minced garlic
½ tsp. mint flakes
½ tsp. sugar
¼ tsp. rosemary leaves
1 bay leaf
  Dash MSG (optional)
2 cups water
3 potatoes, peeled and cut
  in quarters
3 carrots, peeled and cut in
  2-inch slices
2 tbsp. butter
2 tbsp. flour

Slowly brown lamb on all sides in oil. Add seasonings and water; gently simmer 1½ hours or until lamb is almost tender. Add potatoes and carrots. Simmer 40 minutes or until vegetables are tender. In a separate pan, melt butter; add flour and cook until flour is brown, stirring constantly. Stir into stew and cook a few minutes longer to thicken gravy slightly. Serve with noodles, dumplings or hot biscuits. Makes 4 to 6 servings.

CURRIED LAMB CHOPS

Lamb and curry have always made good partners. Here curry and garlic add a distinctive flavor touch to a basting sauce for grilled lamb chops.

½ cup salad oil
3 tbsp. lemon juice
2 tbsp. sugar
2 tsp. curry powder
1 tsp. salt
1 tsp. instant minced onion
1 tsp. seasoned salt
¾ tsp. garlic salt
½ tsp. black pepper
8 lamb chops, cut 1 inch
  thick

Combine all ingredients except lamb chops in saucepan. Bring to a boil, then simmer 10 minutes. Arrange chops on grill 5 to 6 inches from hot coals. Sear on both sides. Continue cooking, basting frequently with the curry sauce, 30 minutes or until chops are browned and done. Makes 4 servings.

MRS. JOSEPH GUBSER'S BARBECUED LAMB

You'll be surprised at the beautiful flavor you can impart to lamb by brushing with a simple combination of garlic and red wine, if you know the right technique.   *Courtesy of: Mrs. Joseph Gubser, Gilroy*

12 to 16 cloves fresh garlic, minced
2 cups dry red wine
Choice young spring lamb, steaks or chops
Salt and freshly ground pepper (optional)
Melted butter or cream

Add garlic to wine. Let mixture stand overnight. Dip or brush (do not marinate) lamb with garlic-flavored wine and allow to stand 8 to 10 hours. Broil quickly over bed of hot coals. If desired, season with salt and freshly ground pepper. Baste with melted butter or cream. The flavor is far superior if cooked over a bed of oak or other hardwood coals.

PORK AND GREEN CHILES

Contrast the richness of pork with a snappy green chile sauce for a delicious, south-of-the-border flavor.
          Recipe contest entry: Pat Haluza, Gilroy

1 to 2 medium-sized onions, coarsely chopped
3 cloves fresh garlic, minced
Olive oil
1 lb. pork, diced
Flour, seasoned with salt and pepper
1 large or 2 small green chiles, chopped
1 can (10 ¾ oz.) chicken broth
1 Jalapeno pepper (optional)
1 large or 2 small fresh tomatoes, chopped
1 tsp. cornstarch mixed with 2 tsp. water

Brown onions and garlic in olive oil. Set aside. Coat diced pork in seasoned flour and brown in the same oil, adding more if needed. After the pork is browned return the onion and garlic to the pan; add the chiles and the chicken broth. (One Jalapeno pepper can be chopped up and added at this time if a sharper taste is desired.) Simmer mixture, and add tomatoes 10 minutes or so before the pork is done. When pork is done, taste for seasoning; adding salt if needed. Stir in cornstarch and mixture and heat until sauce has thickened.

LAMB SHANKS DIVINE

Saucy lamb shanks are tender and tasty from long simmering in a spicy tomato sauce.

    4 lamb shanks
    2 tbsp. flour
1½ tsp. seasoned salt
    ½ tsp. black pepper
    ¼ tsp. MSG (optional)
    2 tbsp. shortening
    1 can (8 oz.) tomato sauce
    ½ cup water
    ½ cup instant minced onion
    2 tbsp. lemon juice
    1 tsp. garlic salt
    1 tsp. sage
    ½ tsp. oregano
    ½ tsp. celery salt

Roll lamb shanks in flour seasoned with seasoned salt, pepper and MSF; brown in hot shortening. Combine remaining ingredients; pour over meat. Cover and simmer gently 1½ hours or until tender. Makes 4 servings.

WAYNE'S BULGOGI   *Korean Barbecue Meat*

In the Vessey household, five or six of these Korean-style marinated flank steaks, fragrant with fresh ginger and garlic, only seem to serve six to eight people. Wayne is a grower and shipper of fresh garlic and his family really knows good flavor and good food.

Courtesy of: Wayne Vessey, Hollister

1½ cups sugar
1½ cups soy sauce
    ½ cup sesame or vegetable
        oil
    20 green onions, minced
    20 cloves fresh garlic,
        crushed
    10 fine slices fresh ginger,
        chopped
    ½ cup sesame seeds
    3 tbsp. pepper
    5 or 6 flank steaks
    Hot cooked rice

Combine all ingredients except steak and rice and marinate steaks in the sauce for 6 to 8 hours (do not refrigerate). Cook over barbecue to desired doneness. Heat remaining marinade and pour over meat and rice when serving.

GILROY—THE
TOWN THAT CLOVE
TO A WINNER
Los Angeles *Times*

MIGHTY GOOD MOUSSAKA

We all know the adage "You Are What You Eat," which happens also to be the title of a food column written by the third-generation winery owner who devised this recipe. If, indeed, we are what we eat, then we can count on being just that much better after a portion of this wonderful concoction of delectable ingredients.

Courtesy of: Louis Bonesio, Jr., Gilroy

2 medium eggplant
½ cup polyunsaturated oil (approx.)
¼ olive oil
1 large onion finely chopped
3 cloves fresh garlic, minced
1 lb. lean ground beef
1 can (8 oz.) tomato sauce
1 large ripe tomato, cut in pieces
1 bay leaf
¼ tsp. Beau Monde seasoning
1 tbsp. honey
¼ tsp. dried oregano
Freshly ground black pepper
10 fresh mushrooms, trimmed and sliced
½ tsp. ground cinnamon
½ tsp. ground allspice
1 cup partially creamed cottage cheese
½ cup dry red wine
¼ cup freshly grated Romano or Parmesan cheese
2 tbsp. parsley, chopped

Peel eggplant and cut into ½-inch slices. In skillet, heat enough polyunsaturated oil to brown eggplant quickly on both sides. Arrange half the slices in the bottom of an oiled 9x12x2 baking pan. Heat olive oil in skillet and cook onion and garlic until golden. Add meat and cook, stirring, for about 5 minutes, breaking up any lumps. In saucepan, heat tomato sauce, fresh tomato, bay leaf, Beau Monde, honey, oregano and pepper to taste. Cook for ten minutes. In separate pan saute mushrooms in a little polyunsaturated oil until golden brown. Add to the meat mixture and mix. Put the chopped meat mixture over the eggplant slices. Sprinkle with cinnamon, allspice and cottage cheese, and cover with remaining eggplant slices. Pour tomato sauce mixture and wine over all and sprinkle with the grated cheese. Bake for one hour at 350°F until top is golden. Remove from oven and sprinkle with chopped parsley. Makes 6 servings.

POULTRY

In ancient times, whole birds were roasted with their cavities stuffed with garlic in a crude attempt to impart flavor and aroma. While this method met with some success, today's sophisticated cook has a wide assortment of foodstuffs with which to vary poultry dishes, and a multitude of cooking techniques to draw upon. Yet garlic still remains a favorite to complement the characteristic good flavor of chicken and other fowl. The recipes included in this section are a good example of the wide range of possibilities, from two elegant game bird recipes and a Gourmet Alley chef's adaptation of Forty-Clove Chicken to a simple broiled garlic and lemon chicken. There's even a recipe for garlic-glazed chicken for a gang.

OVEN-FRIED QUAIL

Here are two tempting recipes for preparing game birds from one of the area's best known hunters—and chefs.

Courtesy of: Peter Moretti, Gilroy

12 quail
1½ cups Sauterne
4 eggs
½ cup milk
1½ cups fine dry bread
    crumbs
2 tsp. salt
1 tsp. pepper
3 cloves fresh garlic,
    minced
⅔ cup butter or margarine

Tie legs of quail together; marinate in Sauterne overnight. Drain and dry thoroughly. Combine eggs and milk. Dip quail in this mixture and in bread crumbs that have been mixed with salt, pepper and garlic. Saute quail in butter until golden brown on all sides. Arrange quail in large shallow baking dish or roasting pan. Cover and bake in 400°F oven 20 minutes until quail are fork-tender.

PHEASANT IN A BAG

1 pheasant
Salt and pepper
Butter
4 cloves fresh garlic,
minced
1 chopped onion

Salt and pepper pheasant inside and out. Rub butter on outside of pheasant and add garlic, onion and a little butter to cavity of bird. Put bird in a brown bag and tie end. Set on cookie sheet and bake 1½ hours at 350°F.

The contest rules specified a minimum of three cloves of garlic in each recipe. "Three cloves," she snorted. "Hah! That's a laugh. I used easily 40 cloves. In the recipe I wrote a whole head, but I just kept chopping until I had a big pile." Curiously the dish was not overwhelmingly garlicky.

HARVEY STEIMAN, San Francisco *Examiner*

KELLY'S ASIAN CHICKEN

This absolutely mouth-watering chicken dish was unanimously selected as the First Place Winner in the Garlic Recipe Contest and Cook-off. It's a simple, inspired combination that takes only 20 minutes to put together. Serve with cooked Chinese noodles and then stand back and let the compliments fly!

Recipe contest winner: Kelly Greene, Mill Valley

3½ lb. frying chicken, cut into serving pieces, or the equivalent in chicken parts of your choice.
3 tbsp. peanut oil
1 bulb (not clove) fresh garlic, peeled and coarsely chopped
2 small dried hot red peppers (optional)
¾ cup distilled white vinegar
¼ cup soy sauce
3 tbsp. honey

Heat oil in large, *heavy* skillet and brown chicken well on all sides, adding garlic and peppers toward the end. Add remaining ingredients and cook over medium high heat until chicken is done and sauce has been reduced somewhat. This will not take long, less than 10 minutes. If you are cooking both white and dark meat, remove white meat first, so it does not dry out. Watch very carefully so that the sauce does not burn or boil away. There should be a quantity of sauce left to serve with the chicken, and the chicken should appear slightly glazed. Serve with Chinese noodles, pasta or rice.

BROILED GARLIC AND LEMON CHICKEN

Just thinking about the tangy flavor of lemon, combined with fresh garlic, can get the juices flowing. Add a hint of oregano and you have a marinade for broiled chicken you'll want to use again and again.

Courtesy of: Karen Christopher, Gilroy

6 oz. lemon juice (use 3 medium lemons)
¼ cup melted butter (or half butter, half corn oil)
3 large cloves fresh garlic, crushed or minced
½ tsp. oregano
Salt and pepper to taste
2 tsp. corn oil
1 3-lb. broiler-fryer chicken, cut into quarters

Mix lemon juice, butter, garlic, oregano, salt and pepper. Preheat broiler and brush pan with 2 teaspoons of oil. Broil chicken, skin side down, for 25 minutes until golden brown, basting with garlic butter sauce. Keep chicken about 12 inches from the source of heat. Turn chicken pieces, skin side up; broil 20 minutes longer, basting frequently, until chicken is fork-tender. Garnish with lemon slices and parsley if desired.

GARLIC CHICKEN WITH ARTICHOKES AND MUSHROOMS

A very elegant dish which draws its subtle, but delicious, flavor from the sweet and rich tasting Marsala wine which is added to complete the sauce. *Recipe contest entry: Carmela M. Meely, Walnut Creek*

8 cloves fresh garlic
¾ cup butter
6 chicken breasts, boned and pounded flat
Salt and pepper
2 tbsp. olive oil
¼ lb. mushrooms, sliced
1 package (9 oz.) frozen artichokes, cooked and drained
1 to 2 tbsp. Marsala, sherry or other white wine
Parsley for garnish

Mince 5 cloves garlic and saute in ½ cup melted butter in skillet; add chicken breasts and sprinkle with salt and pepper. Brown, then remove chicken to a warm platter. Add remaining butter, olive oil and remaining 3 cloves garlic, minced. Brown garlic and toss in mushrooms; add artichokes. Heat. Stir in lemon juice and wine. Let thicken to desired consistency. Pour over chicken; garnish with parsley. Serve with rice.

CHICKEN ROSEMARY

The delicate taste of rosemary gives this dish its distinctive flavor but it's the garlic that adds zest.

1 3-lb. chicken
1 tbsp. flour
5 tbsp. oil
2 tsp. garlic salt
1 tbsp. seasoned salt
1 tbsp. rosemary
¼ tsp. black pepper
1 tbsp. vinegar

Cut chicken in pieces and dredge in flour. Heat 2 tablespoons oil in a skillet, and brown chicken on all sides. Remove chicken from skillet. Brush 1 tbsp. oil over bottom of a shallow baking dish and place pieces of browned chicken close together in dish, skin side down. Combine garlic salt, seasoned salt, rosemary, pepper and remaining oil; brush over chicken. Drizzle with vinegar; cover and marinate in refrigerator several hours before baking. Bake, covered, in 350°F oven 45 minutes. Remove cover and turn chicken to skin side up; then continue baking 20 minutes or until tender. Makes 4 servings.

FORTY-CLOVE CHICKEN FILICE

The Head Chef of Gourmet Alley, who is a garlic grower himself, has his own version of Forty-Clove Chicken which all who have tasted say is fantastic. Don't be timid. To enjoy this dish fully, pull out a hot, juicy garlic clove, hold one end and squeeze it into your mouth, discarding the skin. The garlic will be surprisingly mild, tender and buttery. Ahh . . .!"   *Courtesy of: Val and Elsie Filice, Gilroy*

1 frying chicken, cut in
  pieces
40 cloves fresh garlic
½ cup dry white wine
¼ cup dry vermouth
¼ cup olive oil
4 stalks celery, cut in
  1-inch pieces
1 tsp. oregano
2 tsp. dry basil
6 sprigs minced parsley
  Pinch of crushed red
  pepper
1 lemon
  Salt and pepper to taste

Place chicken pieces into shallow baking pan, skin side up. Sprinkle all ingredients evenly over top of chicken. Squeeze juice from lemon and pour over top. Cut remaining lemon rind into pieces and arrange throughout chicken. Cover with foil and bake at 375°F for 40 minutes. Remove foil and bake an additional 15 minutes.

CHICKEN MAMA'S WAY

Like the classic Spanish dish, paella, Mama's recipe combines chicken, sausage, seafood in a most complementary way.

Recipe contest entry: Ressie Crenshaw Watts, Porterville

½ cup olive oil or cooking oil
4 medium-sized sweet red onions
2 2½-lb. broiler-fryer chickens, cut into pieces
2 cups rice
2 cups chicken broth
2 dozen clams
2 dozen shrimp
1 dozen slices Italian sausage
4 large cloves fresh garlic
1 tsp. saffron
½ cup cooking sherry
Salt and coarsely ground pepper
Pimiento strips
Grated Parmesan cheese

Heat oil in a large casserole. Add onions and chicken pieces. Saute until chicken is lightly browned on all sides; then add rice and 1 cup of the broth. Simmer until chicken and rice are almost tender; add clams and shrimp (if fresh, leave in shells), then sausage. Pound garlic, saffron and 1 cup of broth in a mortar. Strain into casserole and add sherry, salt and pepper to taste. Place strips of pimiento and grated cheese on top. Broil 5 to 8 minutes.

NOFRI'S GARLIC CHICKEN

This crispy-skinned chicken draws its great flavor from slivers of garlic and bits of sage which are inserted into slits in the flesh before cooking. It's easy to prepare.

Recipe contest entry: Jeanette Nofri Steinberg, Santa Monica

1 frying or roasting chicken, whole or cut in pieces
Whole leaf sage
5 cloves fresh garlic, coarsely chopped
Corn oil
Salt and pepper

Rinse and dry chicken. Rub entire skin surface with a clove of garlic. With a sharp knife, make small random punctures in chicken about two inches apart and stuff each hole with a small piece of garlic and some sage. Salt and pepper entire chicken and place in a shallow baking pan. Brush chicken with corn oil and place in preheated 350°F oven for 1½ hours, basting every 20 or 30 minutes.

DIGGER DAN'S CHICKEN

From the proprietors of a Gilroy restaurant who take pride in featuring garlicky dishes on the menu, especially at festival time, comes this recipe for chicken in a garlic, tomato and wine sauce.

Courtesy of: Sam and Judy Bozzo, Gilroy

1 3- to 3½-lb. broiler-fryer chicken
4 cloves fresh garlic, minced
4 tbsp. butter
4 tbsp. oil
Salt and pepper
2 cups white wine
1 lb. ripe tomatoes rubbed through a sieve (or use 1 lb. canned Italian peeled tomatoes)

Cut chicken into quarters. Saute garlic in butter and oil in a large pan, add the chicken legs first and brown them over high heat; then brown the breast pieces. Season with salt and pepper; lower heat and continue cooking until the chicken pieces are tender. Remove from the pan and keep hot. Scraping off bits adhering to the bottom and sides of the pan, stir in the wine and reduce over high heat. Add the pureed tomatoes, salt and pepper to taste; stir well and cook over moderate heat for almost 10 minutes. Return the chicken pieces to the pan, spoon over the sauce and cook for a few minutes longer. Serve the chicken in the sauce.

GIN-GAR CHICKEN

Second place winner in the Garlic Recipe Contest and Cook-off, this recipe combines the flavors of ginger and garlic with yogurt in an unusual marinade for barbecued chicken. Delicious hot or cold.

Recipe contest finalist: Helen Headlee, South San Francisco

8 oz. plain yogurt
8 cloves fresh garlic
1 1-inch square piece ginger root
1½ tsp. chili powder
1½ tsp. salt
1 2½-lb. broiler-fryer chicken cut up (or equivalent chicken parts)

Put a small amount of yogurt in blender; add garlic and ginger and puree until smooth. Remove from blender and stir into remaining yogurt; add spices and blend well. Pour over chicken and marinate in covered container overnight, 12 to 24 hours, shaking occasionally. Cook over hot coals. Serve hot or cold with lemon slices.

FRANCO-SYRIAN CHICKEN

As the name implies this chicken recipe is a combination of French and Syrian cookery. If you prefer, the pine nuts can be ground and used to thicken the gravy. "Serve with French bread and cherry tomatoes" is the recommendation of the chef who created the dish. Definitely a "make it again" meal.

Recipe contest entry: Charles Perry, North Hollywood

1 2- to 3-lb. broiler-fryer
5 cloves fresh garlic
2 large lemons
2 tbsp. oil or clarified butter
1 cup dry white wine
¼ cup *pignoli* (Italian pine nuts)
1 tsp. minced parsley
1 tsp. salt
¼ tsp. pepper

Cut chicken into frying pieces (wings, legs, thighs, deboned breast cut in quarters), discarding neck, back and giblets. Remove fat and skin. Press 3 large garlic cloves through garlic press onto chicken and rub all over with the garlic. Let stand ten minutes. Squeeze juice of one lemon onto the chicken pieces and marinate chicken in garlic and lemon for 20 minutes, stirring once or twice. Wipe garlic off chicken and pat dry with paper towel. Reserve marinade. Fry chicken in oil over high heat, starting with drumsticks, until the meat stiffens and browns. Add wine and marinade and bring to a boil. Reduce and simmer, covered, over low heat for 25 minutes. Meanwhile brown pine nuts: Either put them in 350°F oven for about 20 minutes until they are evenly beige, or fry in a little oil or butter over very low heat, stirring constantly until light brown. When chicken is done, remove and sprinkle with parsley. Keep warm. Add juice of second lemon and one or two more pressed garlic cloves and reduce pan juices over highest heat for 5 minutes. Season with salt and pepper and add pine nuts. Serve chicken with this gravy.

Garlic breathes new life into a town
Washington *Post*

VERMOUTH GARLIC CHICKEN

"With the combination of vermouth and garlic, one needn't worry about garlic odor on the breath," says this chef whose recipe has been in the family for nearly 70 years. Actually when garlic is cooked whole for several hours, as it is here, it loses its pungency and becomes sweet and nutlike in flavor.

Recipe contest entry: France D. Williams, Carlsbad

1 large onion, finely chopped
2 carrots, diced
2 celery stalks, diced
½ small rutabaga, diced
  Large sprig fresh parsley, minced
4 chicken thighs with bone
4 chicken half-breasts, boned
½ cup safflower oil
30 cloves fresh garlic, peeled
  Dry vermouth

Combine onion, carrots, celery, rutabaga and parsley in large bowl and mix well. Remove skin from chicken pieces and wipe with a damp cloth. In large skillet, heat oil and brown chicken pieces on both sides. Start with thighs first as breasts take less time to brown. Drain chicken pieces on paper towels. Spread half the vegetables and half the garlic in a casserole. Arrange chicken on top and cover with the rest of the vegetables and the rest of the garlic. Over entire mixture pour Vermouth and cover casserole. If lid does not fit tightly, cover with foil and then lid. Bake 2 hours in 325°F oven, without removing lid. Serve with French bread on which the garlic cloves can be spread like butter. Delicious! A chilled Chablis is a good accompaniment.

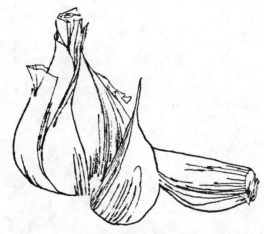

GARLIC WAS THE
STAR OF THE SHOW
Honolulu *Advertiser*

CHICKEN A LA BRAZIL

The use of garlic is a part of almost every cuisine. This recipe calls on Brazil for inspiration, but Brazil, in turn, draws on Africa. No matter the country, garlic and food are good companions.

Recipe contest entry: Lirian Connell, San Rafael

5 cloves fresh garlic
Salt
2 medium-sized onions, minced
1 medium-sized chicken, cut into pieces
2 tbsp. vegetable oil
3 large peeled tomatoes, seeds removed
3 tbsp. chopped green pepper
1/8 tsp. Tabasco sauce
Ground black pepper
2 tbsp. chopped parsley
2 cups whole kernel corn, fresh or frozen

Mash 2 cloves garlic with 1/2 tsp. salt until salt is moist. Add half the minced onion and mix thoroughly. Brush chicken with this paste and let marinate overnight. In frying pan, brown chicken in oil. Remove and set aside. Mince remaining 3 cloves garlic; add to frying pan and brown with remaining onion. Add chicken, cover and cook for 10 to 15 minutes over low heat. Stir occasionally. Add tomatoes, green pepper, Tabasco, salt and pepper to taste, and let cook for about 20 minutes. Add parsley and corn and continue cooking for 10 minutes more. Serve with white rice.

POLLO AL AJULLO

No matter what language you say it in, garlic goes with chicken. In this Latin recipe the sauce is completed with a bit of sherry and thickened slightly before serving.

Recipe contest entry: The Fernandez-Carozzi family, San Mateo

2 medium-sized broiler-fryer chickens
1 cup olive oil
10 cloves fresh garlic, minced
1 large onion, chopped
1 tsp. cornstarch
1 cup sherry
Salt and pepper to taste

Cut up chickens and fry in large pan with olive oil. When chicken is cooked, remove from pan and set aside. Add garlic and onion and saute in oil; when light brown add cornstarch and sherry. Return chicken to pan and let cook another 5 to 10 minutes. Season with salt and pepper.

UNCLE HUGO'S CHICKEN

Uncle Hugo likes his crunchy, garlicky chicken served with corn on the cob, tossed green salad and sourdough French bread with garlic butter. You will, too.   *Recipe contest entry: "Hugo" David Hugunin, San Jose*

⅔ cup dry French bread crumbs
⅔ cup grated Parmesan cheese
¼ cup minced parsley
½ tsp. salt
¼ tsp. pepper
3 cloves fresh garlic, minced
⅓ cup margarine or butter
1 3-lb. broiler-fryer chicken

Mix first five ingredients together in a 1-quart mixing bowl. Set aside. In 1-quart saucepan heat garlic and margarine over very low heat until margarine has melted. Remove from heat. Coat chicken pieces with margarine mixture, then thoroughly coat with crumb mixture. Place coated chicken on large, ungreased cookie sheet skin side up. Mix together any remaining crumb mixture and margarine and sprinkle over chicken. Bake for one hour in 350°F oven. For crisper chicken, cook an additional fifteen minutes.

BURGUNDY CHICKEN MOZZONE

The rich flavor of Burgundy seems to meld all the flavors into one in this recipe which combines green peppers and mushrooms with the chicken.   *Courtesy of: Mary Mozzone, Gilroy*

2 medium-sized chickens, cut in pieces
Flour
4 tbsp. oil
1 can (8 oz.) tomato sauce
½ cup Burgundy
Salt and pepper to taste
Dash of oregano
4 cloves fresh garlic, minced
3 large bell peppers, sliced, seeds removed
1 lb. sliced mushrooms
Fresh parsley, chopped
Parmesan cheese, grated

Dredge chicken with flour and brown in oil. While chicken is browning, mix tomato sauce, wine, salt, pepper and oregano in small bowl. After chicken is brown, put in ovenproof baking dish.

Add garlic to pan drippings and saute ½ minute. Add peppers and mushrooms, stir-fry 5 minutes, then add sauce. Simmer 3 to 4 minutes, and pour over chicken. Cover with foil and bake for 45 minutes at 350°F. Garnish with parsley and Parmesan cheese.

CHICKEN IN GARLIC MUSHROOM SAUCE

A wonderful, rich creamy mushroom sauce turns this garlic chicken into a special event.   *Recipe contest entry: Robin Lee Perkins, Covina*

¼ cup butter
2 tbsp. vegetable oil
1 3-lb. broiler-fryer chicken, cut into serving pieces
30 cloves fresh garlic, minced
1 chopped onion
1 cup dry white wine
¼ cup water
¼ cup milk
1 tsp. salt
Freshly ground pepper to taste
½ tsp. cayenne
1 lb. sliced mushrooms
3 egg yolks
1 cup heavy cream

In Dutch oven or kettle, melt butter with oil on medium heat. Add chicken, brown well, turning occasionally. When brown, remove pieces to bowl. Add garlic and onion to pan and saute until golden brown. Add wine, water, milk, salt, pepper, and cayenne. Stir to loosen browned bits and bring to boil. Return chicken to pan and add mushrooms. Cover and cook at low heat until tender, about 45 minutes to 1 hour. Remove chicken to warm serving plate. Cover with foil and keep warm. Beat yolks into heavy cream until well mixed. Stir into pan drippings. Cook until thickened but do not boil. Spoon some of the sauce on the chicken; offer remainder separately. Serve with rice if desired. Makes 3 to 4 servings.

GARLIC-GLAZED CHICKEN FOR A GANG

It isn't easy to find a party dish that will appeal virtually to everyone, but this one surely will. The chicken takes on a subtle garlic flavor that keeps everyone asking for seconds.

Salt and pepper
40 chicken quarters
2 tbsp. instant granulated garlic
3 tsp. MSG (optional)
2 quarts chicken broth
2 quarts chicken broth
4 cups apricot or peach preserves
2 cups white wine

Salt and pepper chicken and place in baking pan. Combine garlic, MSG and chicken broth. Pour over chicken and bake at 350°F for 1 hour or until tender. Combine wine and preserves, and spoon over chicken. Bake uncovered at 400°F for 15 minutes, spooning sauce over chicken every few minutes. Chicken should have a nice glaze when served. Makes approximately 20 portions.

Seafood

During the Renaissance, banquet guests were requested to compose verses saluting the versatile garlic bulb. We think you'll be composing your own odes to seafood, combined with the goodness of garlic, when you sample the delectable dishes whose recipes are included here. Bass, trout, calamari, scampi, clams and salmon are just a few of the fruits of the sea made worthy of a poet's praise by including garlic in their preparation.

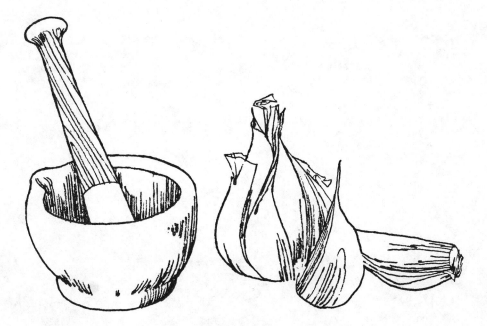

"Sweltering over huge iron skillets, Filice and his chefs dumped in squid by the carton, fresh garlic by the small shovel, fresh tomatoes by the bucket . . . "

MIKE DUNNE, Sacramento *Bee*

CALAMARI, FESTIVAL-STYLE

One of Gourmet Alley's greatest attractions is watching the preparation of calamari. Some argue that eating it is even better. Here is Head Chef Val Filice's recipe for calamari as it is served at the Festival.

Courtesy of: Val Filice, Gilroy

3 lbs. calamari, (squid) cleaned and cut
⅓ cup olive oil
¼ cup white wine
¼ cup dry sherry
1 tbsp. crushed fresh garlic
½ lemon
1 tsp. dry basil or 1 tbsp. fresh
1 tsp. dry oregano or 1 tbsp. fresh
¼ tsp. dry crushed red pepper
Red Sauce (below)

In large skillet heat olive oil at high heat. Add wine and sherry and saute crushed garlic. Squeeze the juice of ½ lemon into pan and place lemon rind in pan. Sprinkle herbs over and add calamari. Saute calamari for approximately 4 minutes on high heat. Do not overcook.

Red Sauce
1 lb. whole, peeled tomatoes, canned or fresh
1 tbsp. olive oil
½ green pepper, chopped
1 stalk celery, chopped
1 medium-sized yellow onion, chopped
3 cloves fresh garlic, minced

Mash tomatoes with potato masher and set aside. In medium-size pan heat oil, add chopped ingredients and saute until onion is transparent. Add mashed tomatoes and simmer for ½ hour. Pour red sauce over calamari and heat for 1 minute.

FAME'S NOTHING TO SNIFF AT IN GILROY
Washington *Post*

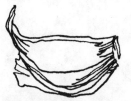

"Garlic-laced specialties were prepared in giant pans from morning to night as wave after wave of festival goers followed their noses to the bustling outdoor kitchen area."

Vacaville *Reporter*

SCAMPI IN BUTTER SAUCE

A festival favorite, Scampi in Butter Sauce is another Gourmet Alley delicacy. The recipe here is courtesy of Val Filice who has served this exceptional dish to the delight of friends and family for years. Scampi, by the way, are a close relative of the shrimp but have no exact equivalent outside Italian waters. Substitute prawns or shrimp of medium to large size.

Courtesy of: Val Filice, Gilroy

Butter Sauce
- ½ to 1 cup butter
- 1 tbsp. finely minced fresh garlic
- 8 oz. clam juice
- ¼ cup flour
- 1 tbsp. minced parsley
- ⅓ cup white wine
- Juice of ½ lemon
- 1 tsp. dry basil
- ¼ tsp. nutmeg
- Salt and pepper to taste
- ½ cup half-and-half

Scampi
- 2 tbsp. butter
- ⅓ cup olive oil
- 1 tbsp. minced fresh garlic
- Juice of 1 lemon (retain rind)
- 1 tbsp. fresh chopped parsley or 1 tsp. dry
- ½ tsp. crushed red pepper
- 1 tbsp. fresh basil or 1 tsp. dry
- ¼ cup white wine
- Dash of dry vermouth
- Salt and pepper to taste
- 3 lbs. deveined and cleaned scampi (prawns)

Melt butter with garlic in small saucepan over medium heat; do not let butter brown. In a separate bowl, mix clam juice, flour and parsley, blending until mixture is smooth. Pour flour mixture into garlic butter and stir until smooth and well blended. Stir in wine, lemon juice, herbs and spices, stirring constantly. Gradually add half-and-half and stir until thickened. Simmer for ½ hour to 45 minutes.

Melt butter in large saucepan on high heat and add oil. Combine remaining ingredients keeping scampi aside until last minute. Add scampi and saute until firm and slightly pink. Do not over cook. Pour 1 cup of scampi butter over scampi. Refrigerate the rest for later use.

G ARLIC'S TIME
HAS COME . . .
Washington *Post*

BASS AND SWISS CHARD

Long a favorite with Europeans, chard is becoming more popular in this country as people begin to appreciate the need to include more dark, leafy greens in the diet. The chard in this recipe helps to keep the fish moist and benefits from the taste imparted by the other ingredients.

Courtesy of: Emma Morretti, Gilroy

2 tbsp. olive oil
1 whole bass, about 4 lbs.
Salt and pepper to taste
2 large bunches Swiss chard
4 cloves fresh garlic, minced
2 medium onions, chopped
2 cans (1 lb. each) solid pack tomatoes

In large covered roasting pan or casserole, place oil and then bass; sprinkle with salt and pepper. Cut chard in 3-inch pieces and lay on top of bass with garlic and onion. Pour tomatoes on top. Bake at 350°F for 1½ hours with cover on. Remove cover and bake another ½ hour. Serve immediately from the baking dish.

SUCCULENT SAUTEED SHRIMP

Shrimp vary in flavor, depending on the area and how fresh they are when served. Garlic is a very good seasoning to use with shrimp whether they are highly flavorful or bland.

1 lb. raw shrimp
¼ cup butter
2 tbsp. lemon juice
1 tsp. parsley flakes
1 tsp. chives
¾ tsp. seasoned salt
½ tsp. garlic powder
½ tsp. dry mustard
½ tsp. tarragon leaves
⅛ tsp. cayenne or red pepper

Shell and devein shrimp. Melt butter in chafing dish or skillet; add lemon juice and seasonings. Saute shrimp in hot herb butter over medium heat 8 minutes or until pink, turning once. Serve hot, preferably on a bed of rice. Makes 2 or 3 servings.

INSALATA DI CALAMARI

The Italians like their calamari deep fried, in seafood stews, in sauces for pasta and in many other popular dishes. It is also absolutely delicious served cold as a tangy fresh salad. This recipe could be served in small portions as an appetizer.   *Courtesy of: John Filice, Aptos*

5 lbs. calamari (squid), cleaned (bodies cut into rings and tentacles separated)
¼ cup olive oil
1 medium-sized bunch parsley, chopped
5 jars (4 oz.) whole pimientos
½ cup olive oil
5 to 10 cloves fresh garlic
1 to 2 cans (2 oz. each) anchovy fillets
Worcestershire sauce
1 tsp. French-style mustard
Red wine vinegar
4 lemons
1 can medium-sized ripe olives

Place cleaned squid in large skillet with natural juices and ¼ cup olive oil. Saute over medium heat until squid is barely cooked, turning frequently. Remove, drain well, and let stand. Chop parsley and pimientos. Pour olive oil into large salad bowl and press half the garlic into the oil. Slice remaining garlic and add to oil. Add anchovy fillets and mash well. Add 2 shakes Worcestershire sauce and mustard. Add red wine vinegar to taste (approximately ¼ cup) and squeeze juice of 2 lemons into mixture. Mix well. Add squid, chopped parsley, pimientos and olives. Toss and refrigerate for at least 5 hours. Mix occasionally. Serve in decorative shallow salad bowl. Garnish with parsley and slices of lemon. Just before serving squeeze 1 or 2 additional lemons on salad.

COCKLES IN GARLIC SAUCE

Though eaten cold with a little vinegar in England and Ireland, Californians like their cockles prepared with . . . you guessed it! Garlic! We think you will enjoy this simple dish.

Recipe contest entry: Donald A. Hunter, Novato

35 cockles (hard-shell clams)
½ yellow onion, sliced in rings
1 cup water
½ cup white wine
4 tbsp. butter
3 cloves fresh garlic, minced
¼ tsp. thyme
½ tsp. minced parsley
1 tbsp. flour, heaping

Steam clams with onion rings, water and white wine until shells open. Remove clam meat and chop well. Reserve 1¼ cups of clam broth. Melt butter and saute garlic. Add thyme, parsley and flour. Stir well. Slowly add reserved clam broth and then chopped clams. Simmer for 10 minutes. Serve over noodles or fresh pasta.

SCALLOPS AND MUSHROOMS BROCHETTE

In some areas fresh scallops are becoming difficult to find and small pieces of shark or other fish are being substituted in the marketplace. Our first choice would be scallops, of course, but this recipe could be used with any similar fish. Be sure not to overcook, particulary if using scallops. They should be slightly *under*done to be at their best flavor.

2 lbs. fresh scallops
½ cup olive oil
2 tbsp. lemon juice
2 tsp. seasoned salt
½ tsp. garlic salt
¼ tsp. black pepper
1 bay leaf
8 coriander seeds
Dash of MSG (optional)
1 can (8 oz.) mushroom caps, drained

Wash and drain scallops and put in flat baking dish. Combine remaining ingredients, except mushrooms, and pour over scallops turning to coat all sides. Marinate in refrigerator several hours. Thread scallops onto skewers alternately with mushroom caps. Place on rack and broil 3 to 4 inches from heat 8 to 10 minutes. Turn and broil 8 to 10 minutes longer. Brush several times with marinade during broiling. Serve with tartar sauce. Makes 6 to 8 servings.

MIXED SEAFOOD SAUTE

Seafood lovers will recognize quickly how good they can expect this combination to be, and indeed it is. Although not a winner in the Garlic Recipe Contest, it merited an Honorable Mention. All who tested it rated it excellent.   *Recipe contest entry: Carmela Meely, Walnut Creek*

½ cup butter
2 tbsp. olive oil
½ lb. raw prawns, shells on
½ lb. scallops
½ lb. crab legs, shells on
⅓ cup chopped parsley
6 cloves fresh garlic, minced
3 chopped shallots
2 tbsp. white wine
2 tsp. lemon juice
Salt and pepper to taste
1 tbsp. sherry or Marsala

Melt butter in pan, and add olive oil. Toss in seafood. When prawns turn pink, add parsley, garlic, shallots, white wine, lemon juice, salt and pepper. Heat through. Stir in sherry. Garnish with lemon slices and serve over rice. Makes 4 servings.

FILLETS NEAPOLITAN

Probably the most famous example of the cooking of Naples is pizza and, although this fish recipe does not contain the cheese usually associated with pizza, it does call for many of the seasonings and familiar tomato sauce, hence the description, Neapolitan.

¼ cup flour
1 tsp. MSG (optional)
½ tsp. salt
¼ tsp. black pepper
2 lbs. fish fillets (sole, flounder, perch, etc.)
¼ cup olive oil
1 cup chopped onion
1 can (8 oz.) tomato sauce
1 can (6 oz.) tomato paste
¼ cup water
2 tsp. parsley flakes
½ tsp. sugar
½ tsp. garlic powder
½ tsp. Italian seasoning

Combine flour, MSG, salt and pepper. Dip fish fillets in seasoned flour, then saute in hot oil until lightly browned on both sides. Remove. Brown onion, then add remaining ingredients. Mix well and simmer 10 minutes. Place fish in sauce and simmer 5 minutes longer or until heated through. Serve with lemon wedges. Makes 4 to 6 servings.

BAKED TROUT MONTBARRY

Mrs. Morretti, whose recipe this is (and whose husband, by the way, is with the Fish and Game Department) did not share with us the secret of the name "Montbarry." However, we are grateful she has shared her most unusual treatment for trout and that we, in turn, can pass it along to you.   *Courtesy of: Emma Morretti, Gilroy*

4 tbsp. butter
1 tsp. parsley, finely chopped
1 tsp. onion, finely chopped
4 cloves fresh garlic, minced
3 heaping tbsp. finely chopped raw mushrooms
6 trout
Salt and pepper to taste
4 egg yolks
3 tbsp. brandy
5 tbsp. soft bread crumbs
5 tbsp. grated cheese (Parmesan or Romano)
Dash of paprika

Using about 1 tbsp., butter a baking dish thoroughly. Line with mixture of parsley, onion and garlic. Sprinkle mushrooms over and place trout which have been seasoned with salt and pepper on top. Pour over 2 tbsp. melted butter and cover the dish with parchment paper (or brown or waxed), heavily buttered with the remaining 1 tbsp. butter. Bake in hot (400°F) oven for 10 minutes. Meanwhile beat egg yolks well; add brandy. Remove paper from trout and pour egg-brandy mixture over. Sprinkle with bread crumbs and cheese, then paprika. Serve in its own baking dish.

TIPSY GARLIC SHRIMP

This sauteed shrimp recipe calls on white wine to make the sauce, and the report is it makes a delightful contribution to the flavor of the dish.   *Recipe contest entry: S. Louise Gershick, Los Angeles*

¼ cup butter
3 cloves fresh garlic, crushed
8 oz. whole mushrooms, stems removed
1 tbsp. lemon juice
12 oz. fresh shrimp, shelled and deveined
1 cup white wine
2 tbsp. cornstarch mixed with just enough water to dissolve

Melt butter in large skillet. Add crushed garlic and whole mushrooms. Gently mix in lemon juice and shrimp. (Add more butter, if needed, at this time.) Saute 1 minute on each side, or until pink. Add wine; increase heat and bring to a boil. Remove from heat and add cornstarch mixture. Return to flame until sauce is thickened. Serve over rice.

CLAMS SAILOR STYLE

Although the author of this recipe says the chopped chile is optional, we recommend you include it, for it gives the dish a most distinctive flavor.   *Recipe contest entry: Fernandez-Carozzi family, San Mateo*

20 medium-size clams
8 cloves fresh garlic, minced
6 tbsp. olive oil
3 tbsp. chopped parsley
2 tbsp. fine dry bread crumbs
Salt to taste
1 cup white wine or sherry
1 chile, chopped (optional)

Soak clams in salty water for 5 hours before preparing dish, and rinse. In a large pan, saute garlic in oil. Add parsley and clams; cover 5 to 10 minutes to open the clams. Once clams are open, add bread crumbs, salt, white wine and chile. Move pan back and forth for about 5 minutes over medium heat until sauce thickens. Makes 4 servings.

RICE A LA NAJAR

Rice can be the star of the meal when cooked to fluffy perfection with chicken stock, tomato juice, garlic and other seasonings. Bright green peas and plump pink shrimp add color and eye appeal.
          Recipe contest entry: Marina V. Najar, Gardena

2 tbsp. corn oil
2 cups long grain rice
3 cloves fresh garlic, minced
3 medium-sized green onions, chopped
1 tsp. vinegar
4 cups chicken stock
1 cup sweet peas
½ cup tomato juice
1 tsp. mustard
Salt and pepper to taste
1 tsp. thyme
¼ cup margarine
2 cups cooked shrimp, cleaned and deveined
Minced parsley for garnish
Paprika for garnish
Pimiento for garnish (optional)

Heat oil in non-stick skillet or pan. Saute rice (do not brown); add garlic, onions and vinegar. Stir gently. Add stock, peas, tomato juice, mustard, salt, pepper and thyme. Stir two or three times gently. Turn heat to medium-high and boil until water comes to about ½ inch above rice. Reduce heat and simmer for about 25 to 30 minutes, or until rice is done. Grains should look whole and be easy to separate with a fork. Dot generously with margarine. Top with shrimp and cover for about 10 minutes. Sprinkle with minced parsley and a little paprika and serve piping hot. Tiny pieces of pimiento can also be used if desired. Makes 6 to 8 servings.

HERB-BROILED SALMON STEAKS

Custom dictates that the cook be gentle when choosing the spices to use in cooking salmon, lest the fish lose its own distinguishing flavor in the process. The seasonings used in this recipe have been carefully selected to blend with and enhance the flavor of the salmon steaks as they broil. However, prejudiced though we may be, the recipe could use just a bit more garlic.

½ cup melted butter
2 tsp. lemon juice
2 tsp. seasoned salt
1 tsp. tarragon
½ tsp. garlic powder
½ tsp. ground marjoram
½ tsp. lemon peel
Dash cayenne or red pepper
2 lbs. salmon steaks

Combine melted butter and lemon juice with seasonings. Arrange salmon steaks on greased broiler rack and brush with one half of seasoned butter. Broil 2 inches from heat 5 to 10 minutes. Carefully turn and brush with remaining butter mixture. Broil steaks 7 minutes longer or until they can be flaked easily with a fork. Serve hot, garnished with lemon wedges and sprigs of parsley.

MOUTH-WATERING BAKED FISH

Jeanne Marks says of her truly mouth-watering baked fish, "The aroma knocks you out." Whole fish are not easy to come by and it's the fortunate chef whose good luck brings him a freshly caught salmon, bass or snapper so he can enjoy this nearly effortless method for cooking it. It is good enough to qualify the author as one of the ten finalists who competed in the Garlic Recipe Contest and Cook-off.   *Recipe contest finalist: Jeanne Marks, Aptos*

8 to 10 lb. whole fish (salmon, sea bass, red snapper, etc.)
Non-stick vegetable spray coating
¼ cup brandy or apple juice
½ cup onion flakes
¼ cup oil or melted butter
¼ cup lemon juice
¼ cup soy sauce
4 cloves fresh garlic, minced or pressed
2 tbsp. Worcestershire sauce
Salt and pepper to taste
Lemon slices
Paprika

Rinse and dry fish and put into baking dish that has been sprayed with a vegetable non-stick spray. Combine all ingredients and pour over fish. Let stand at least one hour. Bake in 400°F oven for about 30 minutes or until fish flakes and has lost its transparency. Baste at least once during baking process. Decorate top with lemon slices and paprika.

BAKED CODFISH GILROY STYLE

There are many different kinds of fish, including codfish, available from nearby Monterey Bay and the Pacific Ocean. This recipe, which includes both potatoes and tomatoes, becomes a meal-in-one. Just serve it with a green salad and your favorite wine.

Recipe contest entry: Aurelia Verissimo, Gilroy

⅔ cup salad oil
4 cloves fresh garlic, crushed
8 sprigs fresh parsley, chopped
6 large new potatoes
2 green onions, chopped
Salt
2 lbs. fresh codfish
1 large tomato
1 lemon
Fresh parsley sprigs

Mix salad oil, garlic and parsley in a measuring cup. Peel and slice potatoes ¼ inch thick. Mix well with ½ garlic mixture and green onions. Spread in a 9x13 baking dish. Salt generously. Bake 20 minutes at 450°F. Remove from oven and place fish fillets on potatoes. Pour remaining garlic evenly mixture over fish. Salt again. Return pan to oven and bake 15 minutes. Garnish with thinly sliced tomatoes, lemon wedges and parsley. Makes 6 servings.

TROUT CANTONESE A LA GOW

One advantage of Chinese cooking is that it preserves the firm texture of fish, and the spices selected tend to highlight the flavor of the fish, bringing all into harmony. Though not traditional by any means, this recipe does call on classic methods and seasonings and produces a fish well worthy of the trout.

Recipe contest entry: Lorraine Soo Storck, Fullerton

2 large trout
1 large bunch scallions or green onions
4 cloves fresh garlic, finely chopped
Fresh ginger root
2 tbsp. soy sauce
4 thinly sliced onion rings
¼ cup bacon drippings
4 large tomatoes
Salt, pepper and garlic powder to taste
1 cup water

Clean and slit trout; place in shallow baking dish. Chop scallions and cover fish. Insert some garlic in slits of fish and sprinkle remainder on top of fish with scallions. Slice thin ginger strips and lay on fish lengthwise. Sprinkle soy sauce on fish. Arrange onion rings in circle around fish. Pour bacon drippings over. Quarter tomatoes and circle fish; season with salt, pepper and garlic powder. Sprinkle water over all; cover with aluminum foil and bake in oven slowly for 1 hour at 350°F. Reduce heat to 275°F and bake for another hour. Baste frequently. Serve with steamed rice. Makes 4 servings.

Miscellaneous

There wasn't a thing that couldn't be cured with garlic, according to ancient folklore. From toothaches, to colds, to the dangers of vampires, garlic was the protector against all evils. While some of its power is now relegated to superstition, garlic still remains the protector against one dreaded problem—the cooking blahs that can overcome even the best of cooks. Garlic's aromatic flavor perks up the tastebuds, banishing boredom while providing infinite ways to add a lively touch to most dishes. From pickles and relishes, to popcorn and chocolate-covered garlic, these recipes are bound to inspire and get those creative cooking juices flowing again.

QUICK AND EASY RECIPE IDEAS

Garlic goes with all dishes, if you give it a chance. Be innovative. Garlic and scrambled eggs? It perks up sluggish morning appetites. Add garlic to soups, salads, and entrees of every kind. And top toast with a garlic spread for a zesty brunch treat.

One recipe contest entrant suggested a flavorful English muffin and garlic treat that is used in her household for colds, flu or bronchitis. Butter toasted English muffin halves and sprinkle with a minced clove of garlic. Spread with grated chese, then top with three more cloves of minced garlic. Broil until cheese melts and the garlic is toasted and crispy. Eat with parsley on the side or sprinkle chopped parsley on top of the muffin before eating. Whether or not these garlic muffins give aid to various ailments, their flavor appeal is likely to perk up poor appetites.

Another contest entrant suggests eating garlic with breakfast cereal. She starts with three small cloves of fresh garlic and chews them quickly. Then she eats the cereal immediately afterwards. "The cereal removes the sting of the garlic and precludes any smell on your breath," she says. Her reason for eating the garlic is to regulate her blood pressure.

SABRINA'S GARLIC SOUFFLE

The youngest entrant in the Garlic Recipe Contest and Cook-off was a teenager whose recipe for garlic souffle qualified her among the ten finalists. Serve for brunch or as an unusual side dish.

Recipe contest entry: Sabrina Vial, Fresno

¼ cup butter
1 can (10½ oz.) cream of celery soup
½ cup milk
1½ tsp. salt
¼ tsp. pepper
2 cups shredded Cheddar cheese
2 tsp. lemon juice
3 beaten eggs
1 cup minced fresh garlic

In large saucepan, melt butter. Add soup, milk, salt and pepper; blend over medium heat until smooth. Slowly add cheese and lemon juice, blending well. Remove from heat; add well-beaten eggs and garlic. Mix well and pour into a greased 1½-quart casserole. Bake uncovered in 350°F oven for 50 minutes.

SUNFLOWER SNAPS

It's a snap to prepare these sunflower nibbles. They are delicious as a snack and also make a crunchy addition to salads, soups, hot cereal or baked beans.   *Recipe contest entry: Camille Russell, Oakland*

1 tbsp. vegetable oil
2 cups raw sunflower seeds, shelled
8 cloves fresh garlic, minced
¼ tsp. salt
1 tbsp. soy sauce

Heat oil in large frying pan over medium-high heat. Add sunflower seeds and garlic. Stir. When a few of the seeds turn golden, reduce heat to medium, and continue stirring as needed. Stop cooking when about half of the seeds are golden. Remove from heat and add salt. After 5 minutes add soy sauce and stir. Store in a jar with a tight lid.

GARLIC-BASIL POPCORN

Popcorn rises to new heights of flavor when tossed with butter, garlic, basil and Parmesan cheese. Whether for TV snacking or as party fare, you won't be able to stop eating these crunchy morsels until they're all gone.   *Recipe contest entry: S. E. Moray, San Francisco*

3 extra-large cloves fresh
  garlic, pressed
2 tbsp. butter or margarine
  Pinch of sweet basil
1 tbsp. oil
¼ cup popcorn kernels
  Salt to taste
2 tbsp. Parmesan cheese

Place garlic in a custard cup, along with butter and sweet basil. Heat a small amount of water in a sauce pan and place custard cup in it to melt butter and infuse it with the herbs, or melt in microwave oven 30 seconds. Heat oil in a heavy iron or stainless steel pot. Drop one kernel in the oil, and when it pops, add the rest of the popcorn and cover. Shake pot now and then as it pops. When all corn has popped, add butter mixture and stir in vigorously. Add salt and Parmesan cheese and stir or shake to coat well.

VESSEY'S DEEP-FRIED GARLIC

Until you've tried these deep-fried garlic cloves, you probably won't believe how delicious they are or how much fun it is to serve them.
                              Courtesy of: Wayne Vessey, Hollister

2 whole bulbs fresh garlic
  Boiling water
1 cup biscuit mix
1 egg
½ cup beer
2 tsp. parsley flakes
½ tsp. salt
  Vegetable oil for deep
  frying

Separate bulbs and peel garlic. Drop cloves into boiling water and, when boiling resumes, blanch for 3 to 4 minutes. The longer the cloves cook, the milder their flavor, but don't overcook, or they will be mushy. Drain and pour cold water over to cool. Meanwhile, prepare batter by combining biscuit mix, egg, beer, parsley and salt. Heat vegetable oil in deep pot or fry cooker. Dip each cooked clove of garlic in batter and fry until golden brown in color. Remove and drain on paper towels. Serve hot.

GARLIC SPICED WALNUTS

One of the long-time fruit crops still being produced in Gilroy is walnuts. The addition of a little garlic flavoring together with ginger and allspice turns them into great between-meal nibbles or cocktail-time snacks.

2 tsp. ginger
½ tsp. allspice
5 cups water
1 lb. walnut halves
4 tbsp. melted butter
¾ tsp. garlic salt

Add ginger and allspice to water and bring to a boil. Drop in walnuts and boil about 3 minutes. Drain well. Spread in a shallow pan and bake in 350°F oven for 15 minutes or until lightly browned. Remove from oven and toss with melted butter and garlic salt.

One good reason for the flourishing garlic industry in California is the warm climate. In such regions garlic develops its best flavor and this is probably why it has always been popular in the cookery which has developed in countries surrounding the Mediterranean. Olives also grow well in such areas, and both garlic and olives are to be found in many fine dishes. Here are two recipes, one hot and the other cold, which combine the flavors of these two products very appealingly.

RIPE OLIVES WITH A HINT OF GARLIC

1 pint ripe olives, with liquid
¼ tsp. (or several shakes) instant granulated garlic
Olive oil

Add garlic to the ripe olives and leave in refrigerator for at least four days. Measure liquid and save half. To this add an equal amount of olive oil. Place olives in this mixture, heat, and keep hot. Serve with cocktail picks.

GREAT GARLIC OLIVES

2 cans (7 oz.) pitted ripe olives, drained
3 tbsp. olive oil
2 large cloves fresh garlic, minced
½ tsp. oregano leaves

Marinate drained olives in the olive oil, garlic and oregano in a covered container for a minimum of 4 hours (the longer, the better).

GARLIC RELISH

Garlic relish adds that extra little touch to dress up simple entrees. With its tomato and eggplant flavor, enhanced with fish paste and garlic, this versatile relish is savory as well as easy to prepare.

Recipe contest entry: Birgita Muller, Los Angeles

1 large or 2 small eggplant
2 large tomatoes
4 cloves fresh garlic
  Salt
1 tsp. fish paste or marmite
1 large onion, thinly sliced
1 tbsp. vegetable oil
1 tsp. brown sugar
2 tsp. chili powder

Slice eggplant, sprinkle with salt and set aside for ½ hour. Cut up tomatoes and remove seeds. Crush garlic and mix with fish paste. Brown onion slightly in oil. Add fish paste, garlic, sugar and chili powder. Add eggplant and mix all together, blending well. Add tomatoes and cook gently for 5 minutes. Taste and add salt if necessary. Put mixture in a bowl in steamer and steam for 20 minutes.

GARLIC DILL PICKLES

When cucumbers are plentiful, put up a batch or two of crunchy dill pickles. They're great for sandwiches and to garnish potato, tuna and other salads.

7 lbs. medium-size
  cucumbers
6 thick onion slices
4 tbsp. dill seed
3 tsp. crushed red pepper
¾ tsp. dehydrated garlic
1 quart vinegar
2 quarts water
½ cup salt

Wash cucumbers and pack into 6 hot sterilized quart jars. To each jar add 1 slice onion, 2 tsp. dill seed, ½ tsp. crushed red pepper, and ⅛ tsp. garlic. For a stronger flavor, use ¼ tsp. garlic in each jar. Combine remaining ingredients and bring to a boil. Pour, boiling hot, over cucumbers, leaving ¼-inch space at top. Seal at once.

PAUL'S PICKLED PEPPERS

If Peter Piper picked a peck of pickled peppers, he'd want to put up a batch with garlic, as in the recipe below.

Courtesy of: Paul Pelliccione, Gilroy

3 lbs. green peppers, (7 to 9 large), seeded
Boiling water
2½ cups distilled white vinegar
2½ cups water
1¼ cups granulated sugar
8 cloves fresh garlic, peeled
4 tsp. salad oil
2 tsp. salt

Cut peppers lengthwise into ¾-inch strips, place in bowl and cover with boiling water. Let stand 5 minutes; drain. Combine vinegar, water and sugar in saucepan; boil 5 minutes. Meanwhile pack peppers into 4 hot sterilized pint jars. To each jar add 2 cloves garlic, 1 tsp. salad oil and ½ tsp. salt. Immediately pour in boiling syrup to cover peppers, one jar at a time. Fill to within ⅛ inch of top. Seal at once. Makes 4 pints.

GARLIC BUTTERS

Garlic butters are easy to make and add an extra-special epicurean touch to many dishes. Slather some on bread slices before adding the filling for rich, zesty sandwiches. Brush loaves of French or Italian bread with garlic butter and broil or bake for mouth-watering garlic bread. Use as a spread to perk up simple canapes.

Melt garlic butter over vegetables or grilled meat for incomparable flavor enhancement or heat some in a skillet to saute shrimp, lamb or other meats or vegetables. Use in sauces, to flavor soups, and don't forget escargots—it's not possible to cook these tender morsels without garlic butter!

Make extra garlic butter to keep on hand in the refrigerator (or freezer for longer storage). You'll be surprised at how many new uses you'll discover if you have some readily available.

Hint: Chill garlic butter, roll into logs, cover with plastic wrap and chill till firm. Slice off as needed.

For a novel party idea, gather friends together to make garlic butter. Everyone can take turns peeling garlic cloves and creaming butter. Each guest will have some nice garlic butter to take home afterwards. What to serve at your garlic party? All sorts of garlicky goodies, of course, from appetizers to salads to the entree, even a garlic dessert if you're daring!

Try one of these combinations for garlic butter.

BASIC GARLIC BUTTER

½ cup butter
2 to 3 cloves fresh garlic,
   pressed or finely minced

Cream butter. Add garlic and beat until fluffy. Makes ½ cup.

Garlic Herb Butters:
Add freshly chopped chives, shallots or parsley to basic garlic butter, or select herbs and spices from the spice shelf—Italian herb seasoning, basil, or dill, for example.

Garlic Cheese Butters:
Add shredded or grated cheese of your choice to basic garlic butter.

Quickie Garlic Butter:
Use ¾ tsp. garlic powder instead of fresh garlic. Add ¼ tsp. salt and a dash black pepper. Let stand for 30 minutes for flavors to blend.

Easy Melt Garlic Butter:
Instead of creaming basic garlic butter, just heat butter and garlic over low heat until butter melts. Do not brown!

Extra Garlicky Butter:
Mash 6 cloves (or use dehydrated equivalent) of fresh garlic into ½ cup butter.

Delicate Garlic Butter:
Blanch and drain 4 cloves of fresh garlic and pound together; combine with ½ cup fresh butter or margarine. Pass the mixture through a fine sieve.

Party Time Garlic Butter:
Moisten 1 tsp. of instant granulated garlic with an equal amount of water. Place in a mixer bowl with 1 lb. softened butter or margarine. Beat until very creamy. Let stand about 20 minutes to blend flavors. Butter may also be melted over hot water or in a food warmer and spread with a pastry brush. Makes enough garlic butter for 100 medium pieces of French or Italian bread or 200 slices of bread or bun halves for sandwiches.

AIOLI

Probably the most famous garlic sauce of all is aioli, the golden, garlic mayonnaise of Provence. So celebrated is this versatile French sauce that certain days are set aside in many villages for feasts that last from noon until after sundown as platters of vegetables, fish, hard-cooked eggs and bread are carried in for dipping up the smooth, garlicky delight.

4 large cloves fresh garlic
2 large egg yolks
1 tsp. dry mustard
¼ tsp. salt
¼ white pepper
1 cup olive oil *
1½ tbsp. fresh lemon juice

* Use half salad oil, if less strong flavor is desired.

Have all ingredients at room temperature. Combine garlic, egg yolks, mustard, salt and pepper in blender jar. Cover and blend at medium speed until smooth. With motor running, remove cover and slowly pour in half the oil in a small steady stream. Stop the motor, and scrape down sides of jar. Cover and turn to medium speed. Uncover and add lemon juice, then remaining oil in slow stream as before, stopping motor to scrape down sides of jar occasionally as sauce thickens. Chill. Serve with hot or cold fish, cold meat or vegetables. Makes 1⅓ cups.

To prepare sauce with hand or electric mixer: Use a narrow deep bowl (a one-quart glass measure makes a good container, or use smaller bowl supplied with larger electric mixer). Beat in oil very slowly, especially at the beginning, being sure oil is completely blended before adding more. When thick, crush garlic cloves over sauce and mix well. Chill.

SKORDALIA   *Greek Garlic Sauce*

A sauce of fresh garlic has been blended together in the Greek islands since the days of the Argonauts, when, it is said, the searchers after the Golden Fleece passed bowls of *skordalia* around their banquet tables. Sometimes nuts are included. Use ⅓ cup blanched almonds, if you like.   *Courtesy of: Katherine Pappas, Gilroy*

6 medium potatoes
4 cloves fresh garlic,
   crushed
2 tsp. salt
1 cup vegetable oil
½ cup white vinegar
3 egg yolks

Boil potatoes and put them through masher as for mashed potatoes. Add garlic and salt and let set for 10 minutes. Using mixer or food processor, mix potatoes and garlic, slowly adding the oil and vinegar, alternating each. (You may add more vinegar if you like a more tart flavor.) After ingredients are thoroughly mixed, add the egg yolks to make the mixture fluffy. Good on bread, crackers and fresh vegetables.

Four good and garlicky barbecue sauces, with any kind of meat.

GARLIC BARBECUE DRESSING

Recipe contest entry: Mirta Richards, Cerritos

2 cups hot water
⅔ cup vinegar
½ cup oil
15 whole peppercorns
10 cloves fresh garlic,
   crushed
4 bay leaves, crushed
1½ tbsp. oregano
1 tbsp. parsley
1 tbsp. salt
1 tsp. rosemary

Mix all ingredients in a jar with a tight-fitting lid and shake well. Refrigerate overnight or longer—the longer the better. Baste meat several times while cooking.

LEO'S GARLIC BARBECUE SAUCE

Courtesy of: Leo Goforth, Gilroy

¾ cup salad oil
¾ cup olive oil
5 cloves fresh garlic, pressed
4 sprigs fresh rosemary
2 tbsp. red wine vinegar
1 tsp. oregano
1 tsp. salt
1 tsp. black pepper
¼ cup lemon juice
1 tsp. Tabasco sauce
1 tsp. Worcestershire sauce

Blend all ingredients 1 hour before using. For chicken and ribs, add 4 tbsp. catsup.

QUICK 'N' EASY BARBECUE SAUCE

1 cup catsup
½ cup wine vinegar
1 tsp. Worcestershire sauce
1 tsp. instant minced onion
½ tsp. seasoned salt
¼ tsp. garlic salt
¼ tsp. barbecue spice
⅛ tsp. black pepper

Combine all ingredients and mix well. Makes 1½ cups.

TERIYAKI SAUCE

1 cup soy sauce
¼ cup brown sugar, packed
2 tbsp. lemon juice
1 tsp. ground ginger
½ tsp. garlic powder
¼ tsp. onion powder

Combine all ingredients in jar. Shake to mix well and dissolve sugar. For a marinade, let stand in sealed jar overnight. Makes about 1 cup.

LOUIE'S SPECIAL MARINADE

If you're lucky enough to have some fresh game, you'll want to marinate it using this special recipe, a delectable blending of flavors.

Courtesy of: Louis Bonesio, Jr., Gilroy

2 cups dry wine
2 cups vinegar
½ cup catsup
2 medium onions,
   quartered and sliced
8 to 10 whole cloves
8 to 10 drops Tabasco
   sauce
4 cloves fresh garlic,
   crushed
3 bay leaves
2 tsp. coarse black pepper
½ tsp. thyme
½ tsp. dry mustard
½ tsp. oregano

Combine all ingredients until well-blended. Do *not* use a metal container for the marinade, but crockery, glass or plastic. The use of so many ingredients may seem wasteful until you realize that the marinade may be used two to three times and that sometimes most of it is used in many recipes. How much or how little you should prepare depends on the amount of meat, so let your experience be your guide. It is advisable to turn the meat occasionally in the marinade.

The marinade may be used for venison and other antlered game, such as elk and antelope, as well as for domestic meats, such as beef and lamb. Most times 24 hours is more than enough for the meat to marinate. If you prefer the gamey flavor, then shorten the time. Since the gamey taste in venison is carried in the fat, it should be removed prior to cooking.

The lean meat should be cooked with a small amount of pork fat, butter or oil to replace the natural fat that has been removed.

SICILIAN GEMS

Chocolate-coated garlic cloves? Why not! The recipe's originator says, "Garlic is very good for you! Particularly for high blood pressure. These little Sicilian Gems are a wonderful way to get your family to eat garlic and enjoy it!

Recipe contest entry: Mrs. Margaret Buccery, Palos Verdes

3 large garlic bulbs (about
  30 cloves)
Ice water
½ lb. sweet dark chocolate
1 tbsp. Grand Marnier or
  liqueur of your choice
  Ground walnuts (optional)

Separate and peel cloves of garlic. Soak in ice water to seal in flavor and juices while you are preparing the chocolate. Melt chocolate in double boiler or fondue pot; add liqueur and blend well. Dry garlic cloves and dip until completely covered in the chocolate/liqueur mixture. Allow to harden, and serve on a small elegant dish at the end of the meal, with cappuccino. These are the "piece de resistance" at the finale of a long and sumptuous Italian meal! (They may also be rolled in ground nuts before they harden, but they are just as good plain.)

Garlic-laced specialties were prepared in gigantic pans from morning to night as wave after wave of festival goers followed their noses to the bustling outdoor kitchen area.

Vacaville *Reporter*

GARLIC PUDDING

During the Garlic Festival, Digger Dan's, a Gilroy restaurant, featured this unusual dessert on their menu. Although the recipe calls for quite a lot of garlic, it is a light and flavorful dessert.

Recipe contest entry: Judith M. Bozzo, Gilroy

2 bulbs fresh garlic
1½ cups cold water
1 cup sugar
1 envelope unflavored gelatin
¼ cup lemon juice
1 tsp. lemon peel, grated
2 egg whites
¼ tsp. nutmeg
 Custard Sauce (recipe below)

¼ tsp. salt
¼ cup lemon juice

Wrap garlic bulbs in foil and bake until done (soft). Remove from foil and boil in water until flavor is transferred from bulbs to water and water is reduced to about 1¼ cups garlic water. In saucepan combine sugar, gelatin and salt. Add ½ cup garlic water; stir until dissolved and remove from heat. Add remaining ¾ cup garlic water, lemon juice and lemon peel. Chill until partially set. Turn into large bowl. Add egg whites and beat with electric mixer until mixture begins to hold its shape. Turn into mold. Chill until firm. Unmold and garnish with sprinkles of nutmeg and custard sauce.

Custard Sauce
4 egg yolks, beaten
¼ cup sugar
2 cups milk
 Dash salt

In heavy saucepan, mix egg yolks with sugar, milk and salt. Cook over low heat until mixture coats spoon. Cool and serve.

Garlic Glossary

SPECIAL TERMS

Bulb. The name for the usable portion of fresh garlic made up of as many as 15 or more individual cloves.

Clove. One of the several segments of a bulb, each of which is covered with a thin, papery skin.

Crushed. A term which refers to fresh garlic which has been smashed by the broad side of a knife or cleaver on a chopping board or with a rolling pin between several thicknesses of waxed paper.

Dehydrated. Any of several forms of garlic from which the moisture has been removed. Dehydrated garlic is available minced, powdered, and granulated.

Fresh. The term used to describe garlic which has not been dehydrated. Actually "fresh" garlic is allowed to "cure" in the field before harvesting just until the papery skin, not the cloves, becomes dry.

Garlic Braid. A garland of fresh garlic braided together by its tops. Braiding is done while the garlic is still only partially cured with some moisture remaining in the tops and before the tops are removed in harvesting. When they become fully dried, they are too brittle to braid. Originally devised as a convenient storage method for garlic that was used in kitchens around the world, braids are quite decorative and have become popular in this country as a kitchen adornment. Serious garlic lovers like to use them for cooking purposes, cutting off one bulb at a time from the braid. Care should be taken if the braid is to be preserved as a decoration that it is not handled carelessly. The papery covering of the bulb is fragile and will break easily when the garlic itself has shriveled after a year or so.

Granulated. A dehydrated form of garlic that is five times stronger than raw garlic. Its flavor is released only in the presence of moisture.

Juice. Garlic juice may be purchased commercially or prepared by squeezing fresh cloves in a garlic press, being certain not to include any of the flesh. Juice blends easily for uniform flavor.

Minced. This term is used for both dehydrated and fresh garlic. Generally called for when small pieces of garlic are desirable as in soups, sauces or salad dressings. Fresh garlic may be minced using a sharp knife on a chopping board. If the recipe calls for salt, add it to the garlic while mincing. It will prevent the garlic from sticking to the knife and absorb the juices otherwise lost in the mincing process. Finely minced garlic, as called for in most French recipes, tends to disappear into the finished dish. For a more robust flavor, mince more coarsely as called for in many Chinese dishes. Large amounts of garlic can be minced using a blender or food processor.

Powdered. Powdered garlic is available commercially. When using powder in recipes with a high acid content, mix with water (two parts water to one part powder) before adding. Powdered garlic can be made from fresh by slowly drying peeled garlic cloves in the oven. When very dry, pound or crush until fine and powdery. Pass through a sieve and pound any large pieces, then sieve again. Store in sealed jars in a dry place.

Pressed. A term for garlic which has been put through a garlic press. There are many different types of presses available, some even "self-cleaning." When using a garlic press, it isn't necessary to peel the garlic clove. Simply cut it in half and place in the press. Then squeeze. The skin will stay behind, making the press easier to clean. Remember to clean your press immediately after use before the small particles which remain behind have a chance to dry.

Puree. A term for garlic which has been cooked at high heat and then pressed through a sieve. Available commercially or made at home, it is excellent to have on hand to blend into soups, sauces or to spread on slices of bread to serve with hors d'oeuvres.

Garlic Salt. Available commercially, it is usually a blend of approximately 90% salt, approximately 9% garlic and approximately 1% free-flowing agent. When using garlic salt in recipes calling for fresh garlic, decrease the amount of salt called for.

Cooking Equivalents Table

Kitchen Measure

      3 teaspoons = 1 tablespoon
     2 tablespoons = 1 fluid ounce
 16 tablespoons = 1 cup
        8 ounces = 1 cup or ½ pound
    16 ounces = 1 pound
         2 cups = 1 pint
        2 pints = 1 quart
        4 pints = 2 quarts or ½ gallon
        8 pints = 4 quarts or 1 gallon
     4 quarts = 1 gallon

Metric Measure

        1 ounce = 28.35 grams
         1 gram = .035 ounce
       8 ounces = 226.78 grams or ½ pound
  100 grams = 3½ ounces
  500 grams = 1 pound (generous)
      1 pound = ½ kilogram (scant)
 1 kilogram = 2¼ pounds (scant)
     ¹⁄₁₀ liter = ½ cup (scant) or ¼ pint (scant)
       ½ liter = 2 cups (generous) or 1 pint (generous)
       1 quart = 1 liter (scant, or .9463 liter)
        1 liter = 1 quart (generous, or 1.0567 quarts)
        1 liter = 4½ cups or 1 quart 2 ounces
     1 gallon = 3.785 liters (approximately 3¾ liters)

Index